Labour Law in Spain

Labour Law in Spain

Fourth Edition

Manuel Alonso Olea†
Fermín Rodríguez-Sañudo
Fernando Elorza Guerrero

This book was originally published as a monograph in the International Encyclopaedia of Laws/Labour Law and Industrial Relations.

Founding Editor: Roger Blanpain
General Editor: Frank Hendrickx
Volume Editor: Frank Hendrickx

Wolters Kluwer

Published by:
Kluwer Law International B.V.
PO Box 316
2400 AH Alphen aan den Rijn
The Netherlands
E-mail: lrs-sales@wolterskluwer.com
Website: www.wolterskluwer.com/en/solutions/kluwerlawinternational

Sold and distributed by:
Wolters Kluwer Legal & Regulatory U.S.
920 Links Avenue
Landisville, PA 17538
United States of America
E-mail: customer.service@wolterskluwer.com

ISBN 978-94-035-3509-8

e-Book: ISBN 978-94-035-3519-7
web-PDF: ISBN 978-94-035-3529-6

This title is available on www.kluwerlawonline.com

The Authors

Professor Dr h.c. Manuel Alonso Olea† (born 19 June 1924) studied law at the University of Madrid, Spain (1941–1946), and obtained his PhD in Law (1951–1953) from the same university. In 1958 he obtained the Faculty of Law Chair of Labour Law at the University of Seville, and in 1965 one of the Chairs of Labour Law of the Faculty of Law at the University of Madrid. He was Letrado at the National Institute for Social Welfare and later Letrado Mayor at the Council of State, in charge of the Labour, Education and Social Security Section of the Council. From 1967 to 1981 he was Chief Justice of the Spanish Central Labour Court and from 1975 to 1993 member of the General Electoral Commission. Professor Alonso Olea was an elected member of the Commission of Social Development and the Commissions of the Economic and Social Council of the United Nations. Several times he was a member of the delegations to the United Nations General Assembly and to the International Labour Organization General Conference. He was acting President and afterwards Honorary President of the Spanish Association of Labour Law and of the Ibero-American Academy of Labour Law and Social Security. He was a numerary of the Royal Academies of Moral and Political Sciences and of Jurisprudence and Legislation. He was Honorary President of the International Society of Labour Law and Social Security.

He was awarded doctorates honoris causa by the Universities of Göttingen, Germany; San Martín, Perú; Central, Dominican Republic; Carlos III, Santiago de Compostela and Leon, Spain.

Professor Alonso Olea wrote more than four hundred articles and essays in Spanish and foreign reviews and lectured in many European and American universities. Among his general books should be mentioned: *Labour Law* (*Derecho de Trabajo*, 22nd edition, 2004); *Introduction to Labour Law* (*Introducción al Derecho de Trabajo*, 6th edition, 2002); *Social Security Institutions* (*Instituciones de Seguridad Social*, 18th edition, 2002); *Procedural Labour Law* (*Derecho Procesal del Trabajo*, 13th edition, 2004); *From Serfdom to Employment Contract* (*De la servidumbre al contrato de trabajo*, 2nd edition, 1987); *Alienation: The History of a Word* (*Alienación: Historia de una Palabra*, 1974). Since 1984 he was editor of Constitutional Court Decisions on Labour and Social Security (Jurisprudencia Constitucional de Trabajo y Seguridad Social).

Professor Alonso Olea died in 2003.

Professor Dr Fermín Rodríguez-Sañudo (born 30 January 1938) studied Law at the University of Seville, Spain (1955–1960), where he obtained his PhD in Law (1971). He has been a Labour Inspector in Madrid (1965–1968) and Seville (1968–1971) and Assistant Professor of Labour Law at the Faculties of Law of Madrid and Seville.

In 1975, he obtained the Chair of Labour Law at the Faculty of Law of the University of Oviedo and in 1976 the Chair of Labour Law of the Faculty of Economics of the University of Seville; since 1998 he has held, the Chair of Labour Law in the Faculty of Law of the University Pablo de Olavide of Sevilla.

His writings include books on the intervention of the state in labour disputes and wages in cases of suspension of the activities of the enterprise; and more than one hundred articles and essays on labour contracts, wages, working time, dismissals, strikes and lock-outs, trade union representatives, collective bargaining, representation of employees in the enterprise, settlement of industrial disputes, labour administration, social security, employment, fundamental rights in the individual labour relation, etc.

Professor Dr Fernando Elorza Guerrero (born 11 September 1970) studied law at the University of Seville, Spain (1988–1993), where he first obtained his degree (with a major in Business Law) and later, in 1999, his Ph.D. in Law. He has lectured at the Faculty of Business and Economic Sciences of the University of Seville (1994–1999) and, since 2002, has been an Associate Professor of Labour Law and Social Security at the Faculty of Law of Pablo de Olavide University (Seville), the institution he joined in 1999.

His research activities have focused mainly on the analysis of collective bargaining in private companies and of corporate restructuring processes, both in their labour and in their social security dimensions. He is the author and co-author of many articles published by scientific reviews and chapters included in collective monographs dealing with these issues. He has also published in the collection of the *International Encyclopaedia for Labour Law and Industrial Relations* (Wolters Kluwer) and other monographs entitled: European Works Council Spain (3nd edition, 2025), and Migration Law in Spain (1st edition, 2019). He is a member of the Spanish Association of Labour and Social Security Law.

Table of Contents

List of Abbreviations

EU	European Union
LRPA	Labour Risks Prevention Act (Ley de Prevención de Riesgos Laborales; Act 31/1995, of 8 November)
LRRDA	Labour Relations Royal Decree Act, (Real Decreto-ley sobre Relaciones de Trabajo; Royal Decree Act 16/1977, of 4 March)
SJA	Social Jurisdiction Act (Ley reguladora de la jurisdicción social; Act 36/2011, of 10 October)
TUA	Trade Union Freedom Act (Ley Orgánica de Libertad Sindical; Organic Acta 11/1985, of 2 August)
WSA	Workers' Statute (Estatuto de los Trabajadores; amalgamated text approved by Royal Legislative Decree 2/2015, of 23 October)

List of Abbreviations

General Introduction

Chapter 1. General Background

§1. Geography

1. Spain, with Portugal the westernmost part of Europe, is geographically and politically formed by the Peninsula and the Balearic and Canary Islands, plus the cities of Ceuta and Melilla on the north African coast.

The peninsula extends over 504,750 sq. km, with a perimeter of 5,849 km, of which 3,904 km is coastline (1,670 km Mediterranean; 1,367 km Atlantic; 867 km from the French border to La Coruña-Cantabric) and 1,944 km are frontier borders with France (712 km) and Portugal (1,232 km).

2. While the border with Portugal is an artificial or historical one, the border with France is quite natural. The Pyrenees, in keeping with a particular preference or interpretation of history, either unite or separate Spain from France, and from Europe generally. However, they were no obstacle for Hannibal on his way from Sagunto to Capua or for the Arabs on their way to Poitiers. Nor, more importantly, were they a barrier against the arrival in the Peninsula of the Celts in prehistoric times, or the successive waves of Germanic tribes in historical years.

That refers only to rather violent episodes of history; to refer to more pacific eras there was, for instance, from the tenth to the sixteenth century, a continuous 'invasion' of peoples from the south of France into Iberia; so much so that the most important ethnic stock in Spain, besides the prehistoric Iberic and Celtic, is that provided by the 'flooding humanity of Gaul', as the economic historian, Professor Vicens Vives, called it.[1]

3. The Balearic and Canary Islands have a coastline of approximately 2,000 km. The peninsula is situated between latitudes 43° and 36° north and 5° and 7° Greenwich longitude West (3° if the Balearic Islands are included). Co-ordinates of the Canary Islands are 25°–27° lat., 9°–14° long.

4. In median altitude, peninsular Spain is the highest country in Europe; 57% of the peninsula is over 600 metres above sea-level and 19% higher than 1,000 metres; but the highest point of Spain is the Teide mountain of Tenerife, in the Canary

1. J. Vicens Vives, *Historia Económica de España*, 4th edn, Barcelona 1965, 29–30; *see* also, on French immigration to Spain, pp. 146 and 384–385.

Islands (3,715 metres); the highest point of the peninsula is the Mulhacén mountain in the Sierra Nevada, Granada (3,478 metres).

5. Historically rather than geographically, the main regions are both Old and New Castile which occupy the central part of the country with an opening to the sea through Santander; León (whose name passim has nothing to do with lions but with the Legio VII Gemina which protected the then quite important sites of gold mines which the Romans exploited through impressive engineering work. Today the ruins, named 'Las Medulas', form a fantastic landscape).

León is to the north-west of Castile where it makes the transition towards Galicia which occupies the Atlantic seaboard north of Portugal. North of Castile and León, are Asturias, the old West Gothic kingdom where the Reconquista began, the Basque country and Navarra, on the Cantabric coast and at the western part of the French border. Aragón, crossed by the Ebro valley, stretches from the central French border down to the south, deep in the Peninsula. Cataluña closes the eastern part of the border with France and opens to the Mediterranean coast; Valencia continues the coastline to the south, to meet Murcia and Andalucía south of Castile, down to the southern Mediterranean and Atlantic coast. Finally, Extremadura extends to the east of the meseta to the Portuguese border. Of course, the geographical peculiarity of the Balearic and Canary Islands also makes these special regions.

6. Perhaps the most important geographical division in Spain is that between 'peripheral' Spain, along the coastlines and including the islands, which is densely populated, either highly industrialized, or with an intensive type of agriculture supported by heavy rainfall or centuries-old irrigation works, or with heavy tourism-related investments, and 'central' Spain, dry, sparsely populated, with farming concentrated on grain and livestock production, and with important tracts of virtually unusable land except, perhaps, for forestry which is subject to heavy fire risk in summertime.

High-range mountains separate the meseta – and divide it into regions – from the coastlines, except towards the west and southwest from where come the only rains to reach interior Spain. Important rivers, except the Ebro, flow westerly across the Peninsula to the Atlantic Ocean; mostly unnavigable, except for a few miles near the sea, they are almost entirely used for hydroelectric power production.

§2. Population

7. The population of Spain according to the 2023 census was 48,196,693 inhabitants, with a predominance of women (24,588,689) over men (23,608,004). The population in 1900 was 18,617,000 and 33,956,000 in 1970. That means that the population in Spain has increased almost threefold throughout the twentieth and twenty-first centuries.

8. The labour force or active population at the end of the first quarter of 2023 has been estimated at 23,580,500. The percentage of the total population which makes up the labour force is lower than in other EU countries (the employment rate stands at 58.52% of the total; 63.65% in the case of men; and 53.79% for women), due to the low percentage of women in the labour force, notwithstanding that it has been increasing in recent years.

The division of the labour force or active population actually occupied between the different economic sectors, again according to the end 2022 estimate, is as follows:

- primary sector (agriculture, forestry and fishery), 6.3%;
- secondary sector (industry, including mining and public works), 20.5%;
- tertiary sector (services), 70%.

9. As in the rest of the European Union (EU) the main trend is the steady decrease of the labour force in the primary sector and the rapid increase of the tertiary sector with the second sector remaining more or less stable.

10. The so-called population pyramid shows a somewhat irregular with a very significant increase in the proportion of older people and a significant decrease in the younger population. The censuses of 1920 and 2022, to compare a more than 100-year demographic span, show the rather different complexions (*see* Tables 1 and 2).

Table 1 1920 Census (Thousands)

Age	*Male*	*Female*	*Total*
Under 5	1,132.3	1,121.6	2,253.9
5 to 9	1,175.2	1,154.9	2,330.1
10 to 14	1,158.8	1,149.8	2,308.6
15 to 24	1,879.7	2,021.7	3,901.4
25 to 34	1,458.9	1,607.5	3,066.4
35 to 44	1,212.2	1,327.4	2,539.6
45 to 54	997.2	1,083.3	2,080.5
55 to 64	772.1	851.8	1,623.9
Older than 65	552.6	664	1,216.6

Table 2 2022 Census (Thousands)

Age	*Male*	*Female*	*Total*
Under 5	929.686	880.082	1,809.768
5 to 9	1,150.375	1,086.536	2,236.911
10 to 14	1,296.012	1,221.361	2,517.373
15 to 24	2,516.815	2,370.817	4,988.972

Age	*Male*	*Female*	*Total*
25 to 34	2,667.410	2,610.431	4,941.672
35 to 44	3,487.636	3,461.087	5,884.263
45 to 54	3,889.290	3,847.571	7,736.861
55 to 64	3,216.751	3,364.817	6,581.568
Older than 65	4,078.098	5,352.077	9,479.010

11. The process of relatively rapid urbanization is also noticeable. In 1900, only four Spanish cities had reached the 100,000 inhabitants mark, while in 2022, there were 64 cities with more than 100,000 people.

12. Urbanization, then, has kept pace with industrialization and development of the tertiary sector of the country.

Distribution between sectors within the country is rather different from province to province. Provinces like Barcelona or Madrid have less than 3% of their population in agriculture, while provinces like Teruel in Aragón, Jaén and Almeria in Andalucía, or Lugo in Galicia have more than 12%; and there is a whole gamut of percentages between these two extreme limits which are inversely repeated in the secondary and tertiary sectors.

§3. Political System

13. Politically Spain is today a parliamentary monarchy. The king, tenant and head of a hereditary monarchy, embodies the Crown. He is the Chief of the State, assumes its highest representation, sanctions and promulgates legislation enacted by the Cortes Generales (Parliament) and is the Supreme Commander of the Armed Forces of the Nation.

14. The legislative power belongs to the Cortes Generales, formed by two Chambers: first, the Chamber of the Deputies (Congreso de los Diputados), today with 350 members elected by the citizens at large under a system of nearly proportional representation; and second, the Senate (Senado) in which sits, at this moment, 74 senators, 4 from every peninsular province, and more severally from the insular provinces and the cities of Ceuta and Melilla.

15. Eligibility for the Cortes and as an elector applies to every citizen of legal age using his or her political rights. Deputies and senators are elected for a four-year period.

16. The executive power is entrusted to the Council of Ministers or Gobierno. It conducts domestic and foreign policy, the civil and military administration, exercises the executive function and the regulation of power.

17. The Government is formed by a Premier, proposed by the king after consultation with the groups represented in the Cortes. Although proposed by the king personally the Premier must have the confidence of the Cortes to carry out any major legislative programme, which means having the confidence of the political party or coalition of political parties which win the election to both chambers of the Cortes Generales. The ministers in charge of the different branches of the government are proposed by the Premier and appointed by the king.

18. The third power of the State, to follow Montesquieu's scheme, is the judiciary, entrusted to a professional, independent hierarchy of judges whose head is the Supreme Court, divided into six chambers; the Fourth Chamber deals with labour and social security cases, on appeals from the lower Courts (as will be seen in detail in Chapter 10).

19. There is no need, we imagine, or space, to delve into the history of Spain, which is as complex and subject to different interpretations as that of other European countries. It is sufficient to say that Spain has accomplished a transition from the authoritarian regime, based upon General Franco's personality and powers, which emerged from the 1936–1939 Civil War to a Western type, democratic political structure for which there are of course historical precedents in Spain. The general legislative elections called for by the Political Reform Act of 4 January 1977 – an Act approved in a national referendum – were duly held on 15 June 1977.

20. The Cortes elected in 1977 projected a new Constitution on 31 October 1978, which was approved by the majority of the Spanish people in a national referendum on 6 December 1978. As with those of many other countries, the Constitution is the first law in the hierarchy of the sources of the law; it is also in labour law, as we will see in the following developments.

21. The latest general legislative elections were called for and held on 10 November 2019. Two strong political forces emerged: the Partido Popular (a centre-right party) and the Partido Socialista Obrero Español (a centre-left party). Under the almost proportional representation system, the Partido Socialista Obrero Español hold 108 seats in the Chamber of Deputies, the Partido Popular 87, and the remaining 155 are divided among a spectrum of parties on the right and left of the political system (Unidos Podemos, Ciudadanos, ERC-CATSI, JxCAT, PNV, EH-Bildu …). In the Senate, the Partido Popular holds 27 seats, the Partido Socialista Obrero Español 31 seats (other parties 13 seats).

§4. Territorial Structure

22. Changes at a political level have produced changes in the territorial structure. The Spanish state has changed from being centralized to more flexible: Article 2 of the Constitution, maintaining the unity of the Spanish nation – and, implicitly, of its state structure – recognizes 'the right to the autonomy for nationalities and regions'. In a process whose commencement was prior to the approval of the Constitution, the different Spanish regions are successively reaching different degrees of autonomy.

The state capital is the Villa (not the City) of Madrid, located almost in the geographical centre of peninsular Spain. Reference has been made to the traditional regions some of which have preserved through the ages their own culture, language and even their own civil law.

23. In this new structure of the state, the regions are Galicia, Asturias, Cantabria, Pais Vasco, Navarra (whose incorporation into the Pais Vasco is still outstanding), Aragón, Cataluña, Castilla-León, Rioja, Madrid, Castilla-La Mancha, País Valenciano, Extremadura, Andalucía, Murcia, Islas Baleares and Islas Canarias. Additionally, two autonomous cities: Ceuta and Melilla.

24. The structure of the autonomous regions, in principle, is an elected legislative assembly, a government and a court of justice. The regional government and its premier are politically responsible to the Assembly. The special rules for each region (Estatutos de Autonomía), enacted by the Cortes Generales, complete its political structure and its competencies. The Constitution contains a list of matters to which the autonomous regions can extend their competencies and a list of the matters that belong to the exclusive competence of the state.

25. Within the regions, the most important divisions are the provinces, forty-seven peninsular and three insular. Each province has a provincial capital whose name usually coincides with the province itself. The provinces have a certain autonomy and are governed by their provincial councils. The state is represented in each region by a Delegate of the Government. Most of the ministries, the Ministry of Labour among them, have provincial administrations.

26. But the basic territorial units are of course the municipal districts urban or rural, all of them having at least one village, town, or city which is the seat of the town council presided over by the mayor. The Constitution guarantees a certain autonomy of the municipality. Members of the council (Concejales) are elected by the residents of the municipal district. The municipalities have responsibility for their own services and have their own fiscal system although their power to tax is strongly limited by the state Acts; in addition, out of its own taxes, the state partly supports the municipal administration. Madrid and Barcelona have special Municipal Acts.

§5. The 'Temporal' Background

27. Before finishing this general background some reference should be made to what may be termed 'the temporal background', meaning the situation of the Spanish system of labour law and industrial relations at the time of writing, which in part relates to changes in the political situation after 1978. The peculiarity of the situation refers mainly to collective labour relations.

28. As far as collective labour relations are concerned and unlike before 1977, trade union freedom and pluralism are today guaranteed by the Constitution. Besides that, employers' associations can also be freely founded. A collective bargaining system is also guaranteed: the bargaining units existing in the old system are not so much modified but the representatives to whom the right to bargain is entrusted and the role of the collective agreement in the regulation of labour conditions certainly are. Relations between employer and employees in the enterprise have been regulated since 1980 in a new way. All these matters are today regulated by the law developing general constitutional provisions.

29. However, the legislation on situations of collective disputes, strike, lock-out, picketing and boycotts, and the settlement of industrial disputes, was enacted before the Constitution came into force: no new laws on these matters have been approved following the constitutional principles. Although a certain clarification has appeared (as we shall see in Part II), several important questions are not as yet definitively resolved. A new regulation could of course resolve them in the near future.

30. With reference to the individual labour relationship or labour contract, the situation as a whole is clearer. The WSA enacted in 1980 is, with multiple modifications as the amalgamated text of 2015, the basic Act in Spanish labour law; other complementary regulations, as we will see in subsequent chapters, have also been approved. The Labour Law Code (Código de Trabajo) announced, at some point, by the WSA, has not been enacted.

31. The 'system' which will be analysed reflects the situation as it stands on 15 July 2023; such precision in a monograph which in part deals with positive law is always necessary; much more so if legal data are changing as they are today in Spain.

Chapter 2. Definitions and Notions

32. Perhaps an indication of Spanish labour law terminology will be convenient at the beginning. Derecho del trabajo (literally labour law) is the expression now almost universally used in Spain. Expressions such as derecho social (social law), derecho obrero (workers, or master and servant, law), derecho industrial (industrial law) sound rather anachronistic and archaic in today's Spain. Labour law is the usual denomination used in academic and general public circles, and the one used by lawyers and specialists, and even allowing for its occasional – or not so occasional – lack of precision, in this matter as in any other, by the so-called mass communication media.

33. The term relaciones industriales (which literally translates the English expression 'industrial relations') is known and used in Spain but in a rather loose sense; it usually covers the same subject matters as labour law, although complemented by an economic and/or sociological point of view. Everyone will understand what is implied when it is used, the implications being, we insist, that underlying the legal principles there is a socio-economic reality.

34. Labour law as an independent branch of law has been long recognized; as a matter of fact, books were written about it before the turn of the twentieth century. The biggest impulses towards its autonomy came from the Workmen's Compensation Act enacted in 1900 and the creation of the Ministry of Labour in 1920. Academic sanction had to wait until 1942 when labour law was formally included as a mandatory discipline in the studies of law in all state universities.

35. As usually taught, though, a big division traverses labour law, on one side of which is individual labour law, dealing mainly with the labour contract, and on the other side, collective labour law. The distinction is not a sharp one; perhaps collective bargaining will be studied within the scope of labour law and collective conflicts as part of the procedures established to settle every type of labour conflict. However, exceptionally, some treatment of trade union law will include collective bargaining.

But usually the expression 'labour law' will include, under various arrangements, both individual and collective labour law (the latter including bargaining, trade unions, strikes, and other types of collective conflict).

36. Perhaps it should be added that labour law has proved itself to be a highly popular branch of law; so much so that in the standard courses of business and economic faculties and schools a course in labour law, generally mandatory, is usually included.

37. A very special situation occurs now with social security law. A labour law professor at the university level is supposed to know and teach it, and so he does, in the regular courses on labour law. But automatically he will start his lecture on this topic by stating that social security law is now so developed that its connections with labour law are few and ever receding. A book on labour law will not normally include coverage of social security law, although some reference will be made to it. Needless to say, all this is in line with the imposing number of social security Acts and regulations; special books are dedicated to its study.

38. Specialists in labour law, or at any rate those who teach it, will think and say that law as a whole can be looked at from the point of view of labour law. Or, rather, that labour law is not only a branch of law but also a way of looking at human exertions from the point of view of law; matters covered by civil or common, mercantile or commercial, procedural, even constitutional or international law will be coloured and illuminated, so to speak, if looked at from this point of view. They will say, for instance, that the most important branch of international law is the law dealing with labour contracts in which the parties are of different nationalities or the contract is executed and/or performed in a country different from that of which the parties are nationals. We will say, too, that you cannot even approach contemporary constitutional law without referring to the right and/or duty to work, the right to unionize and to bargain collectively, the right to strike, the right to some participation in enterprise decisions, the right of the worker to social security and so on.

39. But having said that, the labour law specialist will concentrate on the labour topics or content, collective and individual, referred to above, although not failing to make some incursions into some other branches of the law.

40. Perhaps the incursion will be deepest into procedural law; a full system of labour courts was established in Spain long ago – with, we must say, a fantastic amount of work – and with sections (salas) of Courts of Justice of the autonomous regions and one section (sala) of the Supreme Court dealing with appeals coming from them. All these facts provided for a procedural labour law which is either included in labour law books or subject to special treatment outside the standard procedural law courses and books.

41. Despite all this there is some reluctance to give a definition or even a description of labour law; tentatively it can be said that labour law comprehends within its limits all legal rules and principles that have as a nucleus men or women working for another, and on the institutional set-up in connection with such a situation.

42. Concepts such as, for example, labour court, labour relation, employer, employee, labour council, labour court, trade union, collective bargaining, collective trade agreement, strikes, boycotts, etc., can be the subject of a dogmatic and abstract treatment that will not differ very much from one country to another. There will be differences, of course, in emphasis and detail, but this we think cannot be properly understood out of context. Keeping in mind that a precision about such concepts is necessary in developing the chapters of Parts I and II an effort will be made to give the precision needed and to come down from the abstract to the fully concrete where reality is found and out of which knowledge can be obtained.

43. It is only necessary to add that labour law relies very heavily on civil law concepts as established by a very long tradition of Spanish law whose main foundation was post-classical Roman law, but with some important elements coming from Gothic law, and ancient and immemorial customs coming from a very remote past.

44. The venerable Civil Code contains most of these rules; nobody has to explain within the context of labour law what is meant by a contract, or what is implied in the bona fide performance of a contract, or what damages mean. Nor is it necessary to explain in detail what is meant by an individual or juristic person, or what obligation, right or duty is meant when this term is used. In this sense, it can be said that labour law is a branch which has grown out of civil or common law. But grafts of public law, or considerations of public policy, have been so extensive and intensive that perhaps it can be said, quoting the late and respected Professor Pérez Botija that labour law 'is an indissoluble connubium of Civil and Public Law'.

Chapter 3. Historical Background

45. If the whole phenomenon which is usually comprised within the expression 'industrial revolution' is taken as the beginning of a new era in labour and industrial relations in the wake of which we are still living, then the first observation to be made is that Spain was late, compared with most Western European countries, in feeling the impact of the technological advances which are the core of the revolution.

46. Some beginnings were made, certainly, towards the end of the eighteenth century, especially in and around Barcelona in the textile industries, so much so that as far back as 1790, just a few years after its invention, a contraption was patented in Spain that, according to its description, was most probably a copy of Watt's steam engine. But it came to a sudden and full stop with the impact of the Napoleonic War which from 1808 to 1814 covered almost every corner of Spain, causing a fantastic amount of destruction, and which can only be described as a demographic catastrophe which wiped out almost 20% of the population. There followed almost immediately the American colonial war or, rather, the emancipation of the American colonies, and a profound social and political instability, in which the dynastic problems combined with the difficult transition from an absolute or ancient régime type of monarchy to a constitutional monarchy. Actually, the 'take-off' period of the Industrial Revolution in Spain did not appear until the 1860s, with textiles and railway transport as the leading industries. That being the case, Spain remained a basically agricultural country well into the twentieth century, so much so that in 1900 more than 50% of the population worked in the primary sector, mainly agriculture.

47. Nevertheless, the beginnings of working men's associations could be detected as early as the 1830s and 1840s, although well-organized and established unions did not appear until half a century later. Its late start notwithstanding, this union movement rapidly acquired a very firm foundation, and a rather peculiar anarcho-syndicalist strain, whose very remote roots have to be found in the long and uninterrupted tradition of freedom and individualism of the Spanish worker who, again because of the peculiarities of Spanish history, generally never knew, from the eighth century onwards, the situations of serfdom and forced adscription to the land that are generally described as the feudal system. Through the centuries of the very slow Reconquista the settlers of conquered territories were free peasants, who owned land, singly or in common, with tenures free of feudal duties.[2] Of course, this is only a general outline; isolated pockets of feudalism did exist, coinciding, especially in the south, with a concentration of landed property, but this occurred mostly after the beginning of the fifteenth century, when the Black Death had taken its toll and serfdom was generally on the way to being forgotten all over Europe,

2. An extremely interesting and well documented essay by Professor R. Gilbert, 'El contrato de servicios en el Derecho medieval español (Service Contracts in Spanish Mediaeval Law)', *Rev. Política Social*, no. 101, 1974, covers this long period. Professor Bayón Chacón, *La autonomía de la voluntad en el Derecho del Trabajo* (*Freedom of Contract in Labour Law*) Madrid, 1955, brings the topic up to the beginning of the nineteenth century.

including whatever vestiges of it Spain had known. But again at that time what was really characteristic was not so much a large agricultural sector as the privileged situation acquired by the sheep-raising interests associated with the Meseta, upon which the extremely important international wool trade – and an easy source of revenue for the Crown – was founded; closures were defended precisely against the abuses of the itinerant sheep flocks.

48. To come back to more recent times, from the 1830s to the 1930s the trade union movement took hold among Spain's industrial workers, eventually uniting into large confederations, the CNT (Confederación Nacional del Trabajo) and the UGT (Unión General de Trabajadores), the former with syndicalistic tendencies, the latter with a socialistic approach. The last quarter of the nineteenth century and the first of the 20th witnessed the first modern labour law enactments: hours and conditions of work of minors (1873), workmen's compensation (1900), and adults' maximum hours (1919). The Ministry of Labour was created in 1920; the year before Spain ratified Part XIII of the Versailles Treaty which provided for the creation of ILO and became a member of that body.

49. After the Civil War (1936–1939) an autocratic political system was established; the type of unions referred to were forbidden and organized in lieu of them was a comprehensive and mandatory system of unionization under strong state control and encompassing in the unions both employers and employees. In other words, trade union freedom did not exist in this period; a public system of unionization, besides being mandatory, excluded any other trade unions.

50. The late 1960s and the early 1970s showed the reappearance of unions of Western European type. At first, they were more or less underground, because of the monopoly of representation exercised by the public trade unions organization; they were illegal and existed in especially difficult conditions. Some of them were new in the history of Spanish trade unions, and others were the continuation of historic confederations, as in the case of the CNT and the UGT.

51. In 1977, within the period known as the 'political transition' from the autocratic system to the democratic one, the Trade Union Act implied the recovery of trade union freedom. The up-to-then illegal trade unions became legal, and logically the public structure disappeared, being incompatible with the new conditions.

52. The enactment of the Constitution in 1978 implied the arrival of a new legal framework for labour relations, connecting in a certain sense with the situation previous to the Civil War and General Franco's regime. Besides the guarantee of trade union freedom, it recognized the role of unions and employers' associations in the defence of the interests of employees and employers, the right to strike and the right to bargain collectively. All this, as we have said, occurred in the context of a parliamentary, pluralist and democratic system.

53. More changes, principally due to the economic recession, crisis of employment and technological evolution, occurred in the 1980s and 1990s. Trends towards more flexibility and liberalism in labour relations, mainly in individual labour relations, have introduced important modifications in Spanish labour law in recent years, including the first ones of the twenty-first century. More recently, the Spanish government has implemented consecutive legal reforms in the period 2010–2013, within a programme of reform engaged in by the European Union to deal with the deteriorated economic situation. Both reforms insist on liberalism and flexibility in labour relations. However, at the end of 2021, the Spanish government made up of a left-wing coalition, promoted a labour reform whose main objective was the recovery of labour rights and guarantees by workers. These will be discussed below. In any case, it should be noted that the current status of workers has its origin in the Royal Legislative Decree 2/2015, of 30 October, approving the recast text of the Workers' Statute Act.

54. Reference could be made to some other characteristics of this general background of labour relations. Discrimination based on race, ethnic, religious or similar reasons has never existed in Spain in modern times. Without speaking of discrimination, because that will be a rather inappropriate term, against women, it is a fact that the labour force consists of a higher proportion of men and a lower proportion of women than is customary in a relatively advanced industrial society. Leaving to one side the fact that the situation is changing very quickly, one can generally speak of a disappearing tradition of keeping women away from work, which perhaps was in part a consequence of a very high birth rate – now in a pronounced downward trend.

55. Lastly, we hope not too personal an observation could be the following: the restrictions of trade union and collective rights in the 1939–1977 period were made strangely compatible with a deep and very factual respect for quite wide individual labour rights. Perhaps a good demonstration of this is that Spain, along with France, is the state that has ratified most ILO Conventions (as many as 130 by 2008) and has a very good record of compliance with the high labour standards that the ratified conventions imply (incidentally ILO Conventions nos 87 and 98, on trade union and collective bargaining freedom were not ratified until 1977, almost at the same time as the Trade Union Act was enacted by the Cortes. Also in 1977 the great United Nations human rights treaties – civil and political; economic, social and cultural – were ratified.)

56. Concerning further topics such as the impact of emigration, the highly developed system of Labour Courts and the evolution of the right to strike, the appropriate reference will be made when dealing with them systematically below.

Chapter 4. Role of Government Institutions in the Shaping and Administration of Labour Law and Industrial Relations Policy

§1. THE SHAPING OF LABOUR LAW

57. In introducing the reader to the sources which have shaped labour law we can begin with some general concepts.

Continuously since 1920, there has been, in the Spanish Government, a Department of Labour, or similar (today Ministry of Labour and Social Economy; at the same time, keep in mind that, currently, there is a Ministry of Inclusion, Social Security and Migrations), which has ministerial rank. Prior to this between 1907 and 1920, there existed a public legislatively created body, the Institute for Social Reforms (Instituto de Reformas Sociales). While relatively short-lived, the Institute did some substantial investigative fieldwork on labour conditions and prepared drafts of legal labour law texts, of which ample use was subsequently made.

58. To anyone acquainted with the history of Spanish labour law the role of the Ministry will appear imposing. The reason for this is, on the one hand, that basic formal labour law acts have tended either to expressly allow for delegated legislation – again either to be approved directly by the Minister of Labour or submitted by him to the Council of Ministers – or to implicitly give large leeway to the Ministry for additional or complementary regulations. On the other hand, the Ministry of Labour has approved Labour Ordinances with detailed regulations for the different branches of the economy, today derogated. Latterly, the Ministry has had important faculties to confirm collective agreements and arbitrate in industrial disputes.

59. In the new legal framework after the Constitution we cannot say that the role of the Ministry of Employment as a whole is slight. But it is notably less important than in the previous regime. In connection with the above-related subjects, we may add the following.

60. In the 1980s and 1990s labour ordinances in principle remained in force but were not significant due to the increasing importance of trade agreements. They were definitely derogated on 31 December 1995. The WSA says that regulations of labour conditions by the Government for the different branches of the economy will be made for the sectors and territorial demarcations in which there are no collective agreements, after consultation with unions and employers' associations; extension of a collective agreement in force will be the preferred method.

61. In collective bargaining, the law suppressed in 1980 the ability to confirm the agreement, entrusted in the old system to the labour administration; the agreement gets mandatory force by itself on the basis of the bargaining power to regulate conditions of work. In the matter of settlement of industrial disputes, compulsory arbitration does not currently exist at present, as we shall see below.

62. In wages and remuneration, we must say that, although minimum wages are established in collective agreements, the interprofessional minimum wage is established by the Government after the report of trade unions and employers' associations. Limitations on the increase of wages by administrative decisions have not been made since 1978; as we shall examine below this limitation has been made through agreements between unions and employers' associations, at least until 1983.

§2. The Administration of Labour Law and Industrial Relations Policy

63. Turning now from the 'shaping' to the 'administration' of labour law, the importance of the Ministry of Labour appears again: although its importance is here sharply and extensively curtailed by the very ample jurisdiction of the labour courts. Of course, the courts interpret and apply the law as it is but some case precedent is always involved in the decisions.

64. In addition, it is important to add that the right to autonomy of regions, recognized as we have seen by the Constitution itself, has led to the shaping of a labour administration at the regional level. Their organs have gained many important powers relating to the application of labour law. This distribution of power has reduced in the same proportion the powers of the central administration. Examples of this situation are given later.

65. Given the above and with reference to the section on sources of labour law below, the role of the Ministry of Labour and the regional organs in the administration of labour law and industrial relations can be studied under the following headings:

- the power of inspection;
- the power of sanction;
- the power to decide on certain matters.

66. The organization of the Ministry of Employment to exercise its powers will be examined after the powers themselves have been described.

I. Factory Inspection

67. A factory inspectorate has existed in Spain since 1906, its organization and its faculties have of course changed in almost one hundred years, in accordance with political, economic and social changes and with the role and the shape of public administration itself. ILO Conventions nos. 81 and 129 on factory inspection of industry, commerce and agriculture have been ratified by Spain.

68. The Labour or Factory Inspectorate is attached to the Ministry of Labour. Labour inspectors are entrusted with the authority to visit shops and work centres to see whether or not labour law legislation is complied with. Since the social security system is under the tutelage of the Ministry of Employment, labour exchanges are part of its organization, and migration policies are also within its competence; the Labour Inspectorate is therefore responsible for looking into the compliance of all these with legislation.

69. Labour inspectors are a body of public employees appointed until retirement age. They are all university graduates and are selected on a competitive basis. They discharge their functions through visits or through hearings concerning the parties involved, or both, with the proceedings starting either through complaints or through defects or violations noted by the inspector in the normal discharge of his duties. The labour inspector can either advise or, if there is a clear violation or if his advice had not been followed in due and reasonable time, make his recommendation of a sanction. Sanctions usually take the form of fines; in certain cases, complementary sanctions may be added to them (e.g., loss of subsidies). Exceptionally – in cases of clear and immediate danger of accidents – the temporary or permanent closure of the work centre can be advised and decreed. The labour administration is under a legal duty to send to the criminal courts for their consideration if a crime – or in certain cases a tort – has been committed.

70. Since 1984, labour inspectors have had the cooperation of labour sub-inspectors, also public servants, with functions of help and collaboration in inspectorate activities.

71. In this year, some special rules of regions (Estatutos de Autonomia), now modified, have established their own competence on the Labour Inspectorate. That implies that the unity of the system, until now maintained, may disappear in a few years. A question remains, however: this division seems contrary to the rule of 'a sole central authority' of the Inspectorate according to ILO Conventions. These regional rules have not as yet been applied, except in a single autonomous region; this process therefore is presently stalled.

II. The Power to Sanction

72. In Spanish law, the authority or power to sanction is not a monopoly of courts. It exists to a great extent in administrative organs. This is the case in labour and social matters among others. Of course, it is a power submitted to the law. According to Article 25 of the Constitution, sanctions must be defined by an Act of Parliament.

73. The proposals of the labour inspector recommending a sanction are communicated to the violator, usually the employer, for him to present his allegations and defences in writing. After that, perhaps with some further reports, the matter is submitted for consideration to the executive organ.

74. The power to sanction is today transferred to the labour administration of autonomous regions. In these cases, the decision on fines proposed by labour inspectors is taken by authorities of this regional labour administration.

75. Of course administrative decisions – normally after reconsideration by the administration through an administrative appeal – can be and, very frequently are, appealed to the courts, which have full powers to confirm or to rescind the sanction in whole or in part. Labour Courts have jurisdiction in these cases.

III. The Power of Decision on Certain Matters

76. Occasionally within the labour law system administrative organs are entrusted with powers of adjudication over matters for historical, traditional, or technical reasons. Among the most important of these is the decision about whether there is an economic or technological situation of 'crisis', which allows for the total or partial closing of the work-place with the consequent dismissal of employees when the employer and the employees' representatives do not reach an agreement about this; also the decision on conflicts over the adequate placing of a notice board which the employer must put at the disposal of employee's representatives in the work centre.

77. Administrative organs have similar powers of decision on the temporal closing of the work centre by technological or economic reasons; on the employer's proposal of collective modifications of conditions of work and on the collective transfer of employees to another work centre; and in every case also when employer and employees' representatives do not reach an agreement about these questions.

78. Proceedings vary according to the matter. Generally speaking, a hearing is needed before reaching the decision, an administrative appeal against the decision is allowed and an appeal to the administrative courts is allowed against the final decision. Most of these matters will be taken up again systematically within this monograph.

§3. The Organization of the Ministry of Labour and Social Economy

79. This is a good place as any to deal briefly with this topic. It should be added that this is a risky topic because the organization changes with some frequency! Royal Decree 499/2020 contains the main regulations on the matter, in addition to Royal Decree 139/2020.

80. As the situation stands now, the head of the Ministry or Department of Labour is, of course, the Minister of Employment and Social Security, a member of the Council of Ministers, proposed by the President of the Council and appointed by the King.

81. Currently, the Ministry of Labour and Social Economy has only one Secretary of State: the Secretary of State of Labour and Social Economy

82. The State Secretaries – which is typical for Spanish Ministries – are organized through General Directorates, each of which is headed by a General Director appointed (as are the Under Secretary, the State Secretary and the General Secretaries) by the Council of Ministers upon the proposal of the Minister of employment and social security.

83. Likewise, the Ministry currently has only one General Directorate: the General Directorate of Self-Employed Work, the Social Economy and the Social Responsibility of Companies.

84. Regarding the Labour Inspectorate, its regulatory law, Law 23/2015, of 21 July, created the State Specialized Labour and Social Security Inspection Autonomous Body. This body is part of the Ministry of Labour, and both the General Administration of the State and the Autonomous Communities participate in its Governing Council, as holders of the material powers exercised by the Labour Inspectorate.

85. As to the provincial organization of the Ministry, an 'area of Labour and Migration' exists in each delegation of the Government in autonomous regions.

86. A connection exists between the Labour Ministry and several public institutions in charge of day-to-day operations of matters within the general competence of the Ministry of Labour and Social Economy. Among them, the following should be mentioned:

- the state Public Service of Employment with competences on labour exchanges and benefits for the unemployed;
- the Warranty of Wages Fund whose function in wages payment to the employees will be studied below;
- the National Institute for Safety and Health in the Work Place with competences on investigation of causes of work accidents and professional illnesses, on projects of new measures in this field.

87. As we have seen, autonomous regions with competences in the labour relations field have shaped their own labour administration. Several of them also have their provincial organs.

Chapter 5. Sources of Labour Law

88. On the well-known authority of Professor Castro[3] in starting a discussion of sources of law the distinction is made between the social and political forces that have the power to enact general binding rules, and the ways in which those forces express and externalize their commands.

89. In the first sense, it will be said that the most important labour law source is generally speaking the state, which commands at different levels through different types of organs. The legislative organs either constitutional or normal, will be the typical place of residence of the law-making power of the state. But, on occasions, different organs of the executive power, of the administration, will have delegated or autonomous legislative powers, and the same, with many reservations, can be said of the courts.

These different organs govern through different types of legal enactments; Acts proper, either constitutional or normal; regulations, orders or decrees of the executive; and decisions of the courts.

90. The second labour law source will be said to be the community independently of its formal structures, commanding through the continuity of its conduct to which the *opinio iuris* is added, i.e., the sense and feeling that to proceed and act in a certain way is actually mandatory upon the individual; the community then, speaking through legal custom.

91. To all of which, in the story of labour law shall be added – as one of the most important peculiarities of labour law itself – that new types of measures have appeared along with the state and the community, and along with enactments and customs. Of course, the new powers are the professional associations of employers and employees, and the new measure is the trade agreement reached through collective bargaining. For common and civil lawyers these are most baffling and make for the rather complex problem of the sources of labour law, to which further complexities are added because of the fact that the 'traditional' types of measure tend to specialize in dealing with labour matters, and because of the fact that international rules, rules contained in international treaties duly ratified by the state, tend to have in modern times a high place within labour law.

92. We will try to move through all these complexities, and to give as clear a picture as possible of the sources of Spanish labour law, concentrating on the so-called translative sources, that is, upon the objective measures themselves, leaving as implied the powers from which they emanate.

3. F. de Castro y Bravo, *Derecho Civil de España*, Vol. 1, *Instituto de Estudios Políticos*, Madrid, 1949, pp. 327–328.

§1. THE CONSTITUTION

93. The Spanish Constitution, as we have seen, was enacted by Parliament (Cortes) on 31 October 1978 and approved in a national referendum by the majority of the Spanish people on 6 December 1978. It is the legal text that culminates the transition period from the authoritarian regime to the democratic, pluralistic system.

94. Because of the date of its approval and also because of its content the Spanish Constitution places itself among the 'modern' constitutions. It not only guarantees personal liberties and rights but also establishes principles of substantial equality of every citizen before the law (Spain constitutes a 'social and democratic state of law'); the duty of public powers in order to make effective the liberty and equality of everyone; recognition of organized groups of civil society; recognition of work as a right and duty, as a good especially protected.

95. From a point of view of the general study of sources of law – and of labour law in particular – we must add two points. First, the Constitution is by itself in some subjects a direct source of law; in many others, it contains principles which the future laws must follow and respect. Second, the Constitution rules the rest of the sources of law; both the social and political forces that have the power to enact general rules and the way through which those forces express their commands.

96. Of course we cannot sum up the content of the Constitution, most of its topics are outside the subjects which must be studied in this work. We are obliged however to say something about rules that affect labour law institutions. With this purpose, constitutional rules can be divided into three groups: fundamental rights and public liberties; rights and liberties of the citizens; and principles conducting social and economic policy.

97. In the group of fundamental rights, the following must be mentioned: the duty of the public powers to respect and to promote liberty and equality of man and human groups; the respect of the dignity of the human person; interpretation of rules on essential rights and liberties according to the Universal Declaration of Human Rights and international treaties ratified by Spain; equality for everyone before the law; prohibition of any discrimination for social or personal circumstances; freedom of residence and circulation, free entry and departure from Spain; trade union freedom that contains free foundation and free action; employees' right to strike in defence of their interests.

98. The system of protection that the Constitution provides for this group of rights is especially strong. Regulation of these rights must be made through a special type of law (ley orgánica) of which we will speak later. Against its infringement, there is a special protection appeal (recurso de amparo) before the Constitutional Court and a summary and preferential appeal before ordinary courts.

99. In the group of citizen's rights and liberties, the following must be mentioned. The duty to work, the right to work, free election of profession or trade, promotion through work, right to a sufficient remuneration, prohibition of discrimination by reason of sex, right to collective bargaining between employees' and employers' representatives, right of employees and employers to make use of means of collective conflicts.

100. The rights of this second group can be regulated by ordinary legislation, without the speciality of the ley orgánica; this legislation must in any case respect 'its essential contents'. However, although it does not have the two very special protection means described above for the rights of the first group, its recognition by the Constitution binds the public powers.

101. The third group of rules is, as said before, the conducting principles of economic and social policy. As such the following must be included. The duty to make a policy aimed at full employment; the guarantee of professional training and retraining; the guarantee of security and hygiene in the work and of rest through limitation of working hours and regulation of annual vacation; the maintenance of a public system of social security for everyone; the right to a health service; special protection for handicapped persons and old persons; the guarantee of emigrants' rights and maintenance of a policy aimed at their return.

102. Many of the matters above mentioned merit more attention in other parts of this work, as their intrinsic importance demands. This happens, principally with essential matters of collective labour relations: trade union freedom and trade union-free activity, collective bargaining and collective agreements, and the right to strike.

103. Besides the Constitution proper, there are in Spanish law other formal Acts that, nevertheless, due to the respect they command and the fact that they are the actual foundation of many enactments, can also be called constitutional in a very wide or natural sense. Among them should be mentioned in the first place the preliminary title, Articles 1 to 6 of the Civil Code whose subjects are 'about norms, their application and their efficacy'. The title deals, under that heading, with the sources of law in general, their application and interpretation, their hierarchy, and the basic rules of international and inter-regional law.

§2. Acts of the Legislature

104. As we have said above, the Constitution, besides being a source directly applicable, is the rule which regulates the other sources of law; in the first place, the enactments of the legislature. The following rules are the rules of the Constitution itself, applicable to the law system as a whole, but now treated as sources of labour law.

105. According to the Constitution, we must distinguish two types of law enacted by the Parliament (Congreso de los Diputados and Senado): organic law (ley organica) and ordinary law (ley ordinaria); the latter can be 'direct' legislation or can authorize the executive to regulate certain matters. We will examine both types.

106. The ley orgánica needs, to be approved by the Congreso, a final vote on the whole project with the positive votes of the absolute majority of the Chamber. It is not sufficiently clear if the organic law has a superior rank to the ordinary law: the Constitution requires that the modification or abolition of a law of the first type must be made in any case through another of the same type.

107. Regulation of the 'essential rights and liberties' signalled by the Constitution, above mentioned, must necessarily be done by an organic law. In the labour law field, laws of this type must be those which regulate the trade union freedom and the right to strike. As we shall see below, the first one has been promulgated; on the contrary, the law in force which regulates the right to strike pre-dates the Constitution, and no new one has been promulgated in the constitutional system.

108. The rest of the laws must be qualified as ordinary; they are approved through the normal proceedings established by the Constitution itself for both Chambers: a positive vote of the majority of assisting members provided this number is the majority of the Chambers' members.

109. Normally, these laws are always direct legislation, meaning that enactments that are directly applicable and will be applied by the courts. Executive regulations to implement or to fully develop them will perhaps be needed, but this does not detract from the fact that the Act itself will be directly applied. But Parliament can delegate to the Government the power to give rules with the force of an act of the legislature.

This can be done in two ways. First, through establishing the basic and general outlines of the enactment, and both authorizing and commanding the Executive to regulate by legislative decree, within the limits of the delegation established by the delegating act; this act is not of direct application, as it was said it was a command to the Executive which expires as soon as it is complied with and the delegated act is enacted. Second, through authorizing the executive to recast several acts in one text. Delegated legislation is enacted by the Council of Ministers upon the advice of the Council of the State, a body which prides itself in having some of the best legal brains in the country.

110. In labour law both types of legislation are found. The WSA was a 'direct' type of Act to be applied directly, except when within itself it provides for some delay or further implementation; today it is a delegate Act, where the Government has recast the former text and its successive modifications. Other examples of 'direct' Acts are regulations on temporary work firms, labour risk prevention and employment.

§3. Executive Rules and Regulations

111. Here some very important distinctions have to be made between different norms that, even emerging from the same source, generally the Executive, have different ranks and are actually different one from another because of other characteristics.

112. The first case is the delegated legislation mentioned in paragraph 2 above; there is no need to elaborate on this further.

113. The second case is the decretos-leyes which have the same rank as formal acts of the legislature, although they are promulgated by the Government in the case of 'extraordinary and urgent need'. Within the thirty days following its promulgation, the decreto-ley must be submitted to discussion and voting in Parliament, for its confirmation or abolition.

114. Besides these two special cases, the Government and every Minister have the faculty to make executive rules, general rules in the autonomous competence of the executive power. The norm itself materializes in a Decreto when it emanates from the Council of Ministers; and in an Orden ministerial when it emanates from a Minister. The decretos can be approved to develop or to complement an act or a decreto-ley; they are subordinate to the act they develop, and again prior study and report from the Council of State is mandatory before their enactment.

115. There is some confusion or, at least, there is no clear rule to establish which type of regulations can be dealt with through an order and which need a decree. We will satisfy ourselves by saying that the most important executive regulations such as those that proximately develop an act, are promulgated by decree. Decrees and orders are both legal instruments, although in some cases the Supreme Court has declared an order to be void because of its defect of rank (as they have declared void a decree because of the lack of a previous report of the Council of State).

116. In contrast, there is the distinction between matters which need an act and others which can be regulated by executive rules, because of the principle of 'monopoly of formal act'. In certain cases, the Supreme Court has declared a Decree to be void precisely because of this defect of rank.

117. Executive authorities under the ministerial level are not authorized to enact general regulations, but they do have the power to issue the so-called circulars or instructions to their subordinates on the administrative ladder. The Director Generals, perhaps to reach everyone concerned, publish these types of resolutions in the Official State Bulletin, and they appear to be sources of law, which they are not.

§4. Labour Ordinances

118. Some brief considerations allow us to consider an essential modification produced in the last years in this matter.

119. An Act of 1942 granted a general authorization to the Ministry of Labour to regulate and establish 'minimum conditions' for labour relations between employer and employees 'in the different branches and activities'. As a net result of this Act, labour relations were covered by more than 150 Labour Ordinances for enterprises of all types in agricultural, industrial and services sectors.

120. The enactment of the first Collective Bargaining Act of 1958 forced labour ordinances into the background. A second phase was marked by the enactment of the ES in 1980, which maintained their application until their substitution by collective agreements. The last and definitive phase came when the law derogated Labour Ordinances still in force in 1995.

121. In a certain and very limited sense, the rest of that normative competence exists today. The WSA says that the Government, by a proposal of the Minister of Labour, can regulate conditions of work in the different economic branches. But this power is subject to several conditions. First, that no collective agreement exists in the branch or territorial demarcation; second, that the extension of a previous collective agreement is not possible; and lastly, that the most representative employers' associations and trade unions report on the matter.

§5. Norms of the Autonomous Regions

122. As we have seen, the Constitution recognizes the right to autonomy of regions and that each of them has its own government and assembly.

123. The Constitution establishes that the autonomous region can assume an ensemble of competences, among them of course those of legislative nature. These competences will be regulated in the 'Estatuto de Autonomía', as we have seen, approved by the Cortes through an organic law. Legislative competences for different matters imply the faculty of enacting acts and executive rules.

124. We must add immediately that as far as labour law is concerned, regions do not have these normative faculties. The Constitution says that 'the State has exclusive competence in labour law legislation'; this means that the labour law legislation is the same and unchanging, with no regional differences. Autonomous region organs can have executive authority in order to apply the state laws; the Estatutos of each region include this type of power.

125. Regional governments and assemblies can in contrast, as confirmed by the Constitutional Court, enact acts and executive rules concerning their own administrative organs, i.e., the creation and organization of organs which perform their executive functions mentioned above.

§6. Rules of the Firm

126. According to the same Act that authorized the Ministry of Labour to enact labour ordinances, every enterprise employing more than fifty employees had to discuss with them and later submit for the approval of the Ministry of Labour its formal internal organization rules (reglamento de régimen interior). Collective bargaining, after 1958, stripped these instruments of any importance, since they were born in a time when there was no possibility to bargain collective agreements.

127. The WSA never mentions such internal rules; besides, it abolished the norms that regulated the proceeding to approve them. Thus, a more certain position seems to be that it is not possible to approve new reglamentos (at least with the normative force they had) and that the old ones will be substituted by trade agreements.

128. Of course, what has been said does not mean that the employer is precluded from his faculty to establish general rules of work. What has actually more or less disappeared is the highly formalized form implied by the 'reglamento de régimen interior'.

129. Of course, general orders of the employer must conform to and be within the domain left to the employer by state and collective bargaining regulations; they are not actually a source of law but a part of the individual relationship between the employer and the employee: except in the case where they consolidate, so to speak, past practice or industrial custom, of which more will be said below.

§7. Collective Agreements

130. Collective bargaining or trade agreements form a chapter by themselves, and as such are treated in Part II, Chapter 4. It is enough to say here that a very extensive and highly complex net of collective bargaining agreements covers almost every part of the industry and service sector of Spanish labour relations; and even some parts of agriculture both geographically and by branch. Since 1958, collective bargaining increased its importance as a means of regulation of the conditions of work.

131. In the constitutional framework, as we have said in Chapter 4, the collective agreement has reached a more important role among the sources of labour law's hierarchy. The guarantee of trade union freedom and the right to collective bargaining, established in the Constitution, are essential grounds for this.

§8. Employment Contracts

132. The individual autonomy of the parties, as expressed in the employment contract, cannot generate general rules – Article 1089 of the Civil Code mentioned in the contract between the sources of obligations – but you can create rules to cover the individual employment relationship between the employee and the employer. In this sense, Article 1255 of the Civil Code provides that the contract is 'law between the parties'. Equally, Article 3 of the WSA provides that the employment relationship may be regulated by 'the will of the parties, manifested in the employment contract', provided that the agreed conditions are lawful.

133. In any case, it should be borne in mind that, as provided for in the aforementioned Article 3 of the WSA, the will of the parties as expressed in the employment contract, in any case, to the detriment of the employee, conditions less favourable or contrary not only to the legal provisions but also to the collective agreements in force.

§9. Past Practice

134. Custom is a general source of law, according to Article 1 of the Civil Code; custom is again a source of labour law according to Article 3 of the WSA. 'Custom' in labour law is actually past practice, or as the above-mentioned Article 3 says: 'uses and custom in the locality and of the profession'.

135. Custom emanates from the constant and accepted application of a rule, neither formally enacted nor contained in a collective bargaining agreement. What distinguishes the labour custom and past practice from the civil or common custom is its speciality. No general customs are allowed as a source of labour law, but only customs in a reduced area and for a particular type of work. Custom is actually law in a very proper sense; on the one hand because Article 1 of the Civil Code says that the recourse should be made to custom 'if there is no legal rule applicable' (provided it is not contrary to morals or to public order, and is duly proved); and on the other hand because there are several cases in which the ES refers to custom; amount of work that the employee is supposed to put into carrying out his contract; place and time for paying the wages; term for the termination of the labour contract due to the decision of the employee.

136. The point is that being legally custom, and custom everyone uses and abides by, it is not usual to see it appearing in court decisions; although it does so occasionally. For instance, to quote one case:

> It is a custom in the countryside of Alcaudete de la Jara (a small village in the province of Toledo) that employees in charge of a farm where the employer has provided them with housing accommodation within the farm shall spend the night in the house so provided and within the farm enclosure.

137. In conclusion, custom is a source of labour law but its importance is very secondary because Acts, executive rules and collective agreements cover about every question in labour relations.

§10. Court Decisions

138. The Spanish system of law is not based upon any stare decisis or judicial precedent rule. Court decisions resolve the case at hand, and they are not a rule for further cases with different parties.

139. But that having been said, a highly important point must be added. According to Article 1 of the Civil Code (which settled the common opinion among Spanish jurists), a constant and uninterrupted line of decisions of the Supreme Court establishing a legal principle is a rule of law for every practical purpose, including the possibility of appealing lower court decisions before the Supreme Court if the rule is not followed. These rules are presumably established by the Supreme Court in interpreting the sources of law; and you may properly say that the law, an Act of the Cortes, for example, is the law as interpreted by past decisions of the Supreme Court.

140. Decisions of the Constitutional Court must also be mentioned here because they are highly significant. These decisions are mainly of two types. First, decisions declaring the unconstitutionality of an Act (recurso de inconstitucionalidad) which have general effects according to Article 164 of the Constitution. Second, decisions on the special appeal concerning fundamental rights and liberties (recurso de amparo) whose doctrine has binding effects on all courts. An important number of this second type of decision refers to labour and social matters.

§11. The Hierarchy of the Sources of Labour Law

141. Admittedly this is a rather complex and highly technical topic in every labour law system. We will not say that the problem in Spain is more complicated than usual but some of the most difficult theoretical and practical questions of labour law appear in this field.

142. The root of the complexity can be stated as follows: there is a hierarchical order of sources of law which appears to be firm and almost untouchable, and which actually has these characteristics in the sense that no source can establish labour conditions which are under the minima established by a source which is above it in the hierarchical order. In this particular sense, each grade of the hierarchical order is truly untouchable by lower grades.

143. However, with the provision which will be made, the source actually applicable is that out of the several that may occur, which is the most favourable to the employee. And, in this sense, the untouchable appears touché very frequently and, in fact, a source of law very low in the hierarchical order, appears to be applicable and is applied with preference, leaving aside higher sources.

144. In the first sense it is said that 'the principle of minima' (in Spanish: principio de norma mínima) controls the hierarchical order: no norm can violate minima established by a norm higher in the hierarchical order. In the second sense, it is said that the 'principle of the most favourable norm' (in Spanish: principio de norma más favourable) controls the application of the hierarchical order, the rule to be applied being the one which contains better labour conditions or 'the maximum of the minima'.

145. Bearing in mind the interplay of those two principles – and also bearing in mind what has been said with reference to each type of source – the following is the basic hierarchical order of sources of Spanish labour law:

- the Constitution;
- organic laws, acts of the legislature (ordinary laws); delegate laws and decree-laws, with parity of rank;
- decrees approved by the Council of Ministers;
- sectoral norms approved by the Government after the WSA;
- orders of the Ministers of Labour;
- collective agreements;
- employment contracts;
- custom and/or past practice.

European Union law, directly applicable to every Member State, prevails over national law which is in conflict with EU law. Court decisions permeate the whole system, so to speak, without any definite place within it.

146. At the risk of being tedious we will repeat that in this hierarchy each level establishes minimum conditions for the 'lower orders'; and that the norm to be applied if several of them concur is the one most favourable for the employee. Since the norm lower in rank cannot contain conditions worse than the higher one (because this is a legal impossibility) and will not contain norms equal to the higher (that would be stupid), most probably it will contain better conditions, and so the norm lower in rank will be the one actually applied.

147. Some further application is needed to get to the root of this matter:

- In deciding which norm or source of law contains 'higher' conditions the comparison must be generally made in full, and not point by point, detail by detail. It is for the Labour Court, if the discussion arises, to decide which 'as a whole' is the most favourable norm.
- 'Most favourable' to the employee shall usually be understood in the plain sense of containing better labour conditions. There is, however, a limit on what the lower norms can do to improve. The matter will be taken up again in studying the contents of collective bargaining agreements, but it can be said here briefly

that there are principles of public policy and good faith performance that cannot be infringed upon, no matter how favourable for the employee they appear on the surface.

- Of course, as far as norms of the same rank are concerned the general principle lex posterior lex prior derogat applies to labour law. But perhaps some employees or group of employees can retain old labour conditions, acquired according to an old and now obsolete norm, as a personal right. This so-called principle of 'condición más beneficiosa' has close connections with past practice, and the general trend of the court decisions is that this type of personal conditions shall be maintained unless there is an absolutely clear clause in the collective bargaining agreement renouncing it, and probably offering some compensation because of the renunciation.

§12. General Principles of Labour Law

148. It is a well-settled rule in Spanish law that, to use words of Article 1 of the Civil Code, 'the general principles of law, besides being a general inspiration of the law, will be applied if there is no applicable Act or custom'.

149. After adding collective bargaining agreements to legislation and custom, it should be said that the Courts occasionally make use of the principle pro operario, in their construction of labour law rules, when its meaning has some obscurity, or if there is some doubt about its application to the case in hand. This tends to tip the balance in favour of the employee. Actually, the rule is used with some frequency not in labour cases proper, but in social security cases coming to the help, for instance, of the victim of a work-connected accident or disease, or in favour of his dependants; either, in matters of fact, by displacing the onus probandi onto the employer or his insurer, or, in matters of law, interpreting the applicable rules in a widely 'protective' way.

Part I. The Individual Employment Relation

Chapter 1. Definitions and Concepts

150. The basic individual employment relationship between employer and employee is named in Spain the labour contract or in a literal translation contract of work (contrato de trabajo). Its basic regulations are contained in the WSA.

151. Although the WSA does not contain a precise definition of the labour contract, it may be obtained from the 'domain of application' of the law itself, as follows: the contract that binds the employee who voluntarily provides his services for another person, the employer, within the domain of organization and direction of the latter.

152. An elementary commentary on this definition allows identification of the basic elements of the labour contract:

- The employee offers his services and the services themselves are the object of the contract, not the work done (although the work done is in the background as a consideration or cause of the contract).
- The services are provided voluntarily, a not necessary reference; it is a contract which assumes the parties' consent.
- Every type of service is more or less manual and intellectual, with predominance of one of these elements over the other; but no matter which predominates, there is nothing in the quality of the work which impedes the appearance of the labour contract.
- The employee obliges himself to provide his services, which means he is obliged to work personally.
- The services are paid for, the wages being the payment. Services rendered without payment, because of goodwill or neighbourly relationships, for instance, are expressly excluded from the labour contract or, more exactly, it is said of them that by no means are they labour contracts.
- The services are rendered from the employee to the employer, meaning that the employer has, by virtue of the contract, a right to those services and to whatever is the product, material or 'intangible', of the services in question.
- Lastly, the services are rendered within the domain of the organization and direction of the person to whom the employee offers his services. The actual formulation of what has been traditionally qualified as 'subordination' of the employee;

this element must be understood in a legal sense, with a certain flexibility, especially in certain services and works, which imply a degree of autonomy of the employee.

153. In any case, more recently, Spanish law has incorporated a specific reference to the presumption of labour contract of certain jobs carried out in the field of digital platforms. Specifically, Spanish law establishes that it is presumed to be included in the scope of application of the WSA, and therefore it is considered labour unless proven otherwise that shows that in the specific case we are not dealing with a labour contract, the activity of people who provide paid services consisting of the delivery or distribution of any consumer product or merchandise, by employers who exercise the business powers of organization, direction and control directly, indirectly or implicitly, through the algorithmic management of the service or the conditions of work, through a digital platform.

154. It is not necessary to say that the legal definition – or, in the past, those contained in other laws – has been developed through hundreds of court decisions which have evolved through time, the general tendency being to relax the sense of subordination. This coincides with the legal definition above in which the mention of subordination has disappeared in a flexible form. Some measure of subordination is still deemed to be necessary in order to have a labour contract and not an individual contractor.

155. The usual distinction is logically made between the contract out of which the relation emerges, and the relation which develops the promises of the contract, but the expressions (individual) labour contract or relation are interchangeable in common and even in legal use.

§1. The Different Categories of Employee

156. Explicit in the WSA is the difference between a normal or general labour contract and a series of special labour contracts ('special labour relationships' are the words of Article 2 of the WSA). Additionally, this same legal norm excludes from its scope of application a set of work activities, taking into account the lack of some of the elements that characterize the employment contract (Article 1.3 WSA). Finally, we must also consider the existence of a whole set of labour relationships with particularities and, therefore subject to specific rules.

I. Special Labour Relationships

157. The specialism refers mainly to the type of work done in complying with the contract, which of course has a close relation with the employee himself. So, to speak of special labour contracts is to speak of special categories of employees.

158. The WSA authorizes the Government to regulate these special relationships, that have been made since 1985. Obviously, this regulation separates itself from the WSA but not absolutely, its rules frequently serve as a general pattern and also as supplementary law.

A. High Ranking Personnel

159. The work of those the WSA qualifies as 'high ranking personnel', people, other than the employer himself, placed high in the hierarchy of the enterprise merit a special study. A threefold distinction should be made:

a. Persons who are members of the board of corporations. They do not have labour contracts, and the WSA excludes them from its domain.
b. Persons who are not members of the board but still have wide and ample responsibilities for the company or enterprise as a whole or some important work placed within the enterprise. Up to 1976, they were excluded from the Labour Acts and regulations; an Act of 1976 included them as a special labour relationship, a qualification confirmed by the WSA.
c. Other 'high ranking personnel' but without general powers, and subordinated to some general director. Their contracts are deemed to be common labour contracts, the concept of 'high direction personnel' being exceptional and to be restrictively construed.

160. The announced special regulation is today the Royal Decree 1382/1985, 1 August. It establishes that high-ranking personnel are employees who have general powers in the enterprise, with autonomy and responsibility only limited by the instructions of its superior organ of administration. The contract must be in writing. The time of work will be fixed by the parties, and may not be manifestly superior to the usual time for other employees. Apart from the general cases of disciplinary dismissal, the contract may terminate because the decision of the employer notified the employee within a three-month term. High-ranking personnel are neither elected nor eligible in the representative organs of the employees in the enterprise.

161. A certain number of court decisions have outlined the concept and applied the special regulation to the personnel. The main aspects of these decisions refer to distinction from other personnel also placed in the first level of the enterprise but considered common employees; and to termination of the contract by the decision of the employer.

162. In recent years, several judicial decisions have established the difference between a high-ranking labour contract and the labour provided by a society partner; this one does not imply a labour relation, nor either the work of the member of the board of the corporation, a relation of commercial nature, even though it includes administration or management functions. Court decisions have maintained also that the status of society partner and high-ranking personnel is not compatible when capital participation is especially significant or effective control exists over the society. Nor is the high-ranking contract compatible with the status of a member of the board of the corporation. Finally, the same person cannot be at the same time a high-ranking person and a common salaried employee, the first being a subject with autonomy and full responsibility and the second a subordinate person.

B. Domestic Services

163. Nobody has doubted that the relationship between the domestic servant and the person to whom these services are rendered is a labour contract. Up to 1976, however, it was excluded from labour legislation; at this moment, an Act qualified it as a 'special labour relationship', which WSA confirms. In passing it can be said that the number of domestic servants has decreased and is decreasing very rapidly, especially traditional domestic servants living at home with the family to which their services are rendered.

164. The Royal Decree 1620/2011, of 14 November, regulates this special labour relationship. The more important features of this regulation are the following: the contract can be concluded for an indefinite period or for a specific duration; the inter-professional minimum wage is applicable (obviously the parties can fix a higher wage); housing, maintenance and other goods can cover a part of the remuneration, up to 30% of the total salary. Apart from the general causes of termination of the contract, it may be terminated by the unilateral decision of the employer, notified to the home servant within a twenty-day or a seven-day term, depending on the duration of the contract itself.

C. Convicts and Minors under Preventive Detention

165. This special labour relationship is regulated by Royal Decree 782/2001, of 6 July. The services of the convict are placed under the direction of a public administrative office, which assumes the role of the employer. Basic rights of the employee – among them, remuneration and minimum rest – apply to the labour relationship. General labour law regulation only applies when an express remit is made.

166. Apart from this special relationship, there are 'non-productive works' in prisons, as well as the so-called works for the benefit of the community, as a form of serving sentences, and which do not generate an employment relationship. Finally, we must also consider the existence of works performed by convicts authorized to leave the prison temporarily for an employer, and which, in this case, are regulated by the WSA.

167. In a similar way to what happens with convicted persons, the WSA considers a special labour relationship that of minors, under preventive detention, who carry out paid work as part of the fulfilment of their criminal responsibility. In this case, the minor must be sixteen years old, and the provision of paid work will be governed by both Royal Decree 782/2001 and Royal Decree 1774/2004.

D. Professional Sportsmen

168. Reference should be made, because the problem has been much debated, by professional sportsmen, especially professional football players, football being the most popular sport in Spain. Football and other professional players of sport (jai-alai, golf, cyclists) were completely excluded from the labour contracts and were submitted to the rules established by their 'federations', which in fact were, and are, federations of clubs, that is, of employers. There was a provision that no player could even appear before a court of law and that he should submit every difference with his club to arbitration proceedings provided by the Federation. But a very important 1971 decision of the Central Labour Court (later followed by several decisions of the same court and of the Supreme Court) ruled that the arbitration rule was null and void because it took away from the players their basic right as citizens to plead their cases before the courts, and it also declared that their relations with their clubs were labour contracts.

169. In 1976, an Act regulated their work as a special labour relationship, which the WSA maintains. The announced special regulation has been promulgated: the Royal Decree 1006/1985, of 26 June, which says that professional sportsmen are those who practise regularly a sport for another person and within the domain of organization and direction of a club or institution and are paid. The most important particulars of this regulation are: the duration of the contract (always for a limited period of time, although an extension of time is legal), the possibility of a cession from one club to another, termination of the contract. General rules of labour law apply as supplementary. Of course, the EU Court doctrine in the Bosman case applies in Spain.

E. Artists in Public Spectacles

170. In the evolution of the rules approved before the WSA, qualification of this work as a labour contract offered some problems, especially regarding persons considered 'leading figures'. Today their consideration as a labour contract presents no problem and covers artists who carry out their activity in the performing, audiovisual and musical arts, as well as people who carry out technical or auxiliary activities necessary for the development of said activity.

171. The Royal Decree 1435/1985, of 1 August regulates this special labour relationship. The contract must be in writing; it can be for a limited or an indefinite period of time. Working time includes the effective activity of the artist before the public and time dedicated to essays. There are special regulations for weekly rest and holidays. Norms of the Civil Code are applicable in case of breach of the contract by one of the parties. General rules of labour law apply as supplementary.

F. Salesmen

172. The inclusion of this professional group in the domain of labour law has had a long process. Court decisions did not consider it as a labour contract, at first because these persons work under no conditions of subordination. In 1962, the law included them in the domain of labour law, provided they follow the instructions of the employer, the employer has the final say on the contract tentatively agreed upon by the traveller and the traveller is not responsible for the success or the failure of the contract. The WSA includes them among the special relationships and requires only that the traveller is not responsible for the success or the failure of the contract; thus probably a further step has been made in the way of amplification of the domain of this special professional group.

173. The special regulation announced by the WSA has been promulgated by a Royal Decree 1438/1985, of 1 August. Its most important aspects are: contract in writing, right of the employee to recognition by the employer of the clientele obtained through his work, and damages for dismissal which can be increased according to the number and importance of the clientele. Wages are usually paid in the form of commissions and they are regulated with some detail.

G. Handicapped Persons

174. An Act of 29 November 2013, on the rights of persons with disabilities and their social inclusion (Royal Legislative Decree 1/2013), has recognized the contract of handicapped persons who are employed in special centres as a special labour relationship, which the WSA today confirms.

175. This contract is regulated by Royal Decree 1368/1985 of 17 July. Special provisions refer to limitation of working time, kind and amount of work, wages, paid absences to attend rehabilitative treatment and professional readaptation, suspension and termination of the contract due to inability of the employee.

H. Sanitary Services Personnel

176. Act 44/2003, of 21 November on Sanitary Professions Regulation has added a new special labour relationship, of sanitary personnel (doctors, pharmacists among them) receiving special training in public or private centres.

177. This special relationship is regulated by the Royal Decree 1146/2006 of 6 October. Some aspects of its regulation (such as its duration, work time, period rest or the termination of the contract) are conditioned by the purpose of training due to the employee. These and other general rules apply as complementary norms.

I. Barristers at Collective Law Offices

178. Royal Decree 1331/2006 of 17 November regulates the special relationship of barristers who provide their services, with a salary, within the domain of organization and direction of a law office. The subordination implied in this contract is notwithstanding compatible with a certain degree of autonomy in the professional providing of the work.

179. Labour provided to other employers than a collective law office is excluded from this special labour relation: this is also the case with services rendered by barristers not paid with salaried fees and collaboration between barristers.

180. General rules of the WSA, such as trade union freedom, safe conditions of work, the right to strike, protection of wages and others, act as supplementary norms, where they are compatible with the special nature of the special relationship. Besides general causes of termination of the contract, breach of mutual bona fides and loss of professional ability must be added.

II. Labour Relationships with Particularities

A. Distant Work

181. The labour relation denominated as 'contract at the employee's home' has been replaced since 2012 by the 'distant work contract'. Its special note is the place where the employee provides his work, the employee's home or a different place decided by him. Other substantial features of this relation are the same as the common labour relation.

182. Regulated by Act 10/2021, of 10 July, this Act focuses on regulating remote work – a form of work organization or carrying out the work activity in accordance with which it is provided at the worker's home, or in the place chosen by it, during all its day or part of it, on a regular basis – considering teleworking – that remote work that is carried out through the exclusive or prevalent use of computer, telematic and communication media and systems telecommunications – as a modality of that.

183. The contract must be in writing, the employer must inform the employee about vacant work places at the work centre; he must also establish appropriate measures to assure his access to professional training, in order to allow him his professional promotion. In any case, the worker cannot be forced to provide work under this modality, requiring his consent to do so.

184. These employees have the same rights as those who provide their services in the work centre, except those inherent to work in the enterprise. The law expressly refers to adequate protection in work security and rights of collective representation in the work centre; the employee must be assigned to a determined work centre of the enterprise.

185. Collective agreements, especially in certain activities, are beginning to include rules on this type of work; they develop and complete the limited legal prescriptions.

B. Longshoremen

186. Work of loading, unloading, stowage and transfer of merchandise in ports is not from 2017, under the Royal Decree-law 8/2017, of 12 May, a special employment relationship, although it was considered such until that date. This legal norm has brought about a profound reform of the legal regime of this activity, which has its origin in a Court decision of the EU Court of 2014, which condemned Spain for violating its legislation, in this case, the freedom of establishment recognized by the Community Treaties.

187. This activity is regulated, today, in addition to the above-mentioned Royal Decree-law, by Royal Legislative Decree 2/2011, of 5 September, and the Royal Decree 371/1987, of 13 March. One of the principles enshrined by the new legal regime established in 2017 is the freedom of the recruitment of port employees for the provision of the service port for the loadings of merchandise, previously non-existent. In any case, the application of the ordinary labour regime is supplementary to the specific legislation mentioned above.

III. Activities Excluded from Workers' Statute Act

A. Public Employees

188. Article 1.3 of the WSA excludes from labour legislation the work of employees who serve public bodies, in principle regulated by administrative law. But these bodies can have labour contracts, namely for temporary work, auxiliary or complementary activities or special works. Common or general labour law applies to them, with some particularities derived of course from the nature of the employer.

189. Having said that we must add that actually, looking at the type of work done, almost every labour contract is different or special with reference to another in a different industry or trade. These are dealt with through collective bargaining agreements. But the differences do not alter the fact that we find ourselves within the confines of a labour contract as defined at the beginning of this chapter.

B. Obligatory Services

190. The exclusion of this type of activities by Article 1.3 WSA, is a consequence of the lack of voluntariness that characterizes this type of activities. Today, obligatory services, in our law, have been reduced to cases of serious social risk, public calamity or catastrophe, such as those provided for by Organic Act 4/1981.

C. Director or Member of the Board of Directors

191. Article 1.3 WSA excludes from its scope of application the activity that is limited to the mere performance of the position of director or member of the administrative bodies of companies that have the legal form of an enterprise, provided that their function within the company only involves the performance of tasks inherent to their position. The reason for this exclusion is the absence of subordination at work since the typical function of these people is the representation and direction, at the highest level, of the company.

192. The relationship of these people with the companies, whose board they are part of is, established through a commercial contract. Only in the case of small companies, such as family companies, have the Spanish courts admitted that they can carry out work of an ordinary nature, and therefore have, at the same time, a labour relationship.

D. Benevolent, Friendly or Good-Neighbourly Works

193. The reason for the exclusion of these types of works is that their cause is not profit, but mutual help or altruistic collaboration.

194. In the case of work based on friendship or good neighbourliness, these are usually sporadic collaborations, so that, if the service is sustained over time, there may possibly be an indication of another type of relationship, more typical of a labour contract, especially if financial compensation is given. With regard to benevolent work, if remuneration finally exists, the possible existence of a labour relationship, and, therefore, of a labour contract, would also have to be considered.

E. Family Works

195. The exclusion of family jobs is established in the WSA, specifying the legal norm that this will be the case unless the status of employees of those who perform them is demonstrated. This exclusion has its origin in the consideration that there is no employment relationship in the work performed.

196. However, this is an exclusion that is not total, as it does not cover any relative or family member of the businessman. Specifically, it only affects the spouse –

not the de facto partner – descendants, ascendants and other relatives by consanguinity or affinity up to and including the second degree, and, where appropriate, by adoption. In addition, these relatives are required to live with the employer.

197. The work that is subject to exclusion in this case is that which is carried out for companies that are individually owned, or that take the form of a community of property. Therefore, the assumption of companies with a corporate form is ruled out.

F. Commercial Operators on Behalf of One or More Employers

198. This exclusion occurs when autonomous commercial agents or operators are obliged to be responsible for the successful completion of the operation, assuming the risk thereof. It is then considered that there is a commercial relationship.

199. However, the Spanish courts have considered it possible for the same person to maintain at the same time an employment relationship and a commercial relationship with the same company if activities of both types are compatible.

G. Transportation Services

200. There are three requirements for transport services to be excluded from the scope of application of the WSA, and therefore the existence of a commercial transport contract must be assessed:

a. That the carrier is the owner of the transport vehicle, or that by any other means (lease, loan, etc.) has the power to dispose of it.
b. That directly offers its services to the public or the market.
c. That he is the holder of an administrative transport authorization (transport card).

201. In any case, the Spanish courts have considered the existence of administrative transport authorization as a determining element for exclusion from labour legislation.

H. Self-Employment

202. Self-employment is a type of work that is performed without subordination to the orders or instructions of another person, and this is an element that justifies its exclusion from the scope of the WSA.

203. However, the WSA contemplates that a legal norm expressly provides otherwise, which has allowed some labour laws to be applicable to this type of work – for example, in terms of trade union freedom or labour risk prevention.

204. A specific category in the field of self-employment is economically dependent self-employed workers, who have their own legal regime. According to Spanish legislation, such will be considered a self-employment worker who carries out an economic or professional activity for profit and in a habitual, personal, direct and predominant manner for a natural or legal person, on whom he or she depends economically for receiving from him, at least, 75% of their income from earned income and economic or professional activities.

I. Other Services That Do Not Have a Labour Nature Either

205. Article 1.3 WSA finally excludes all work that is carried out in the development of a relationship other than what is considered an employment relationship, as defined in WSA (Article 1.1).

206. One of the assumptions that fits into the provision of Article 1.3 WSA is the case of fellows, as people who participate in a training activity frequently in exchange for remuneration. Sometimes, it is not easy to differentiate a fellow from a worker, especially when the fellowship is used to disguise a genuine employment relationship.

207. A different assumption from the previous one, but which is also affected by the exclusion established by Article 1.3 WSA, is the case of people who carry out training internships, within the framework of a training program or an external internship program. However, once again we must note the existence of situations in which, by participating in a training program, one is ultimately faced with an employment relationship: the clearest example is the training and work experience contracts or the special employment relationship established between certain health personnel in training and public or private health institutions, to which we have referred before.

§2. The Individual Labour Contract

208. Probably the most important criteria for the establishment of some classification within the labour contract are those which refer to the duration of the contract itself.

I. Duration of the Contract

209. The general rule of Spanish labour law has been that the labour contract was for an indefinite period of time. The rule was not based on any theory of freedom of contract and it was not the result of some implied will of the parties; rather the principle should be construed (especially after 1976) in the sense that some objective factor or element must be present to allow for a contract for a limited period of time.

210. In the WSA, the labour contract for an indefinite period of time and the contract for a limited period of time seem to be considered equally; the parties can choose one or the other. We must say, however, that the general rule favourable to the first type of contract remains in the WSA; the parties may limit the duration of their contract, again, only if some objective factor or element is present. This approach has been reinforced after the 2021 labour reform, which has clearly limited the cases in which recourse to fixed-term contracts is possible.

211. These objective factors or elements are actually listed in the WSA: (a) circumstances of production, whether it is an occasional and unpredictable increase in activity, or an occasional and predictable increase in said activity, which has a limited duration in the time; (b) workers employed as substitutes for other workers who are absent for some special reasons (sickness, work accident, covering a job while the selection or promotion process is taking place, etc.).

212. In 2021, the possibility of entering into labour contracts to carry out specific works or services was eliminated from the WSA. This legislative novelty must be placed within the framework of a determined policy of reducing the cases in which fixed-term contracts can be made and aims to induce greater stability in the employment of Spanish workers.

213. Special reference must be made to seasonal work for certain activities, mainly in agricultural or tourist-connected activities; here has appeared the so-called permanent-discontinuous type of worker, meaning that an employee who, during several past seasons, has actually worked for an employer has a legal right to be offered re-employment for the next and subsequent seasons. Technically this is a contract for an indefinite period of time. The contract must be in writing, the rights of the employee are the same as the rights of ordinary employees. The employer is obliged to contact the worker when the activity of the enterprise begins again.

214. In any case, the 2021 labour reform has increased the cases in which this type of indefinite contract can be concluded, thereby exceeding what could be considered its traditional framework. Specifically, the WSA contemplates that this contract can be concluded to:

a. the performance of works of a seasonal nature or linked to seasonal productive activities – this was the ordinary assumption;

b. the development of works that do not have said nature but that, being of intermittent provision, have certain, determined or indeterminate execution periods;
c. the execution of work consisting of the provision of services within the framework of the execution of commercial or administrative contracts that, being foreseeable, form part of the ordinary activity of the company.

Additionally, the WSA establishes that this contractual modality may be concluded between a temporary employment company and an employee to be transferred to another company in which they temporarily provide their work.

215. As we have seen, the general rule of the law is for a labour contract to be for an indefinite period of time and there exists a list of limited contracts. Consequently, all contracts illegally limited are deemed to be for an indefinite period of time. Notorious cases of fraud, so qualified by court decisions, are first, the agreement to work for a limited period of time when the work place is a permanent feature of the enterprise; second, a succession of temporary contracts with the same employee.

216. Of course, the indefinite duration does not mean that the contract cannot be terminated for any reason, but the causes of termination belong to the theory of dismissals and are also applied to contracts of limited duration (they will be studied in Chapter 6 below).

II. Temporary Work

217. Temporary work firms are regulated by Act 14/1994 of 1 June. Brief consideration must be given to the legal status of these firms, the labour contract between them and the employee and lastly the contract between the temporary work firm and the user of the temporary employee.

218. Temporary work firms need special authorization from the Ministry of Labour or the administrative organ of an autonomous region. It must provide a financial guarantee to ensure the fulfilment if its obligations as an employer (mainly payment of salaries and social security contributions). It is required to engage in the sole activity of supplying temporary work. The authorization will expire when the firms stop carrying out the activity consisting of making workers available for one year without interruption.

219. In the case of serious violations of its labour duties, a temporary work firm can be sanctioned with the termination of the authorization as a temporary work firm. However, later the temporary work firm could request a new authorization.

220. The temporary work firm is looked upon as the employer of the temporary employee. The labour contract may be for an indefinite or definite period of time and out of it emerges a common labour relationship. The temporary work firm may celebrate contracts for the training and contracts for the practical work (for these types of contracts *see* below Chapter 7, §3) with the employees who will work for the user enterprise; also fixed-term contracts, when the causes that justify them exist (*see* Article 15.2 WSA), and labour contracts of a fixed-discontinuous nature. The employer assumes the principal duties arising from the contract, i.e., remuneration, professional training and social security contributions. The employer also has disciplinary powers. This labour relationship obviously has some special elements, but the WSA does not qualify it as a special labour relationship.

221. Temporary work firms are obliged to assign yearly 1% of their wages to the professional training of their temporary employees. They must communicate to the administrative organs notice of employees working at the user firm.

222. The contract between the temporary work firm and the user of the temporary employee is a *sui generis* one, always for a specific period of time to cover the user's temporary need for labour. It must be put in writing. The user assumes certain managerial powers (direction and control of the provided work) and obligations (safety and hygiene). The employee has the right to wages established by the collective agreement of the temporary work firm or of the user. When the employee continues to provide his services to the user beyond the termination of the contract between the two employers he will be deemed to be an employee of the user for an indefinite period of time.

223. In September 2016, the EU Court delivered three decisions in which it was established that the Spanish labour law was in breach of EU rules on temporary labour recruitment and temporary appointments of employees in the public sector. Specifically, the EU Court considered that the Spanish legislation violated Directive 1990/70/EC. For these purposes, it is considered that it was not in conformity with Community law to treat employees with a temporary contract less favourably, at the time of termination of the employment contract, than permanent employees.

224. Equally, the EU Court considered that the status of the temporary employee does not have a legal justification when the appointments of these employees are spread over a number of years. In these cases, the posts that these employees hold should go out to public tender for their proper provision, it is not possible, in the meantime, for the employment relationship to be extinguished unilaterally by a decision of the employer.

225. As a consequence of this jurisprudence, in 2021, the Spanish legislator modified Article 15 WSA, reducing the cases in which recourse to fixed-term contracts would be possible, established new criteria regarding concatenation of contracts, while eliminating the possibility of celebrate, from now on, contracts for a specific work or service.

III. Trial Period

226. Until 1976 no general provision for a trial period existed. Nevertheless, it appeared in almost every branch of industry either in the labour ordinances or in collective agreements. An Act of 1976 'legalized', so to speak, the trial period, establishing some general rules that the WSA virtually repeats today.

227. These general rules of the WSA are as follows:

a. The duration of the trial period shall be specified by collective agreement. If this is not the case, the rule of the WSA applies, it shall not exceed six months for technical personnel or two months for other personnel (three months in the second case in enterprises of less than twenty-five employees). In the case of the contract for a limited period of time (Article 15) not longer than six months, the trial period may not exceed one month, except when the collective agreement orders something different.
b. The agreement on a trial period shall be in writing; if it is not, it shall be considered not existing at all.
c. During the trial period the employee has the same rights and duties as any other employee; and if the trial period ends without any of the parties withdrawing from the contract, the time is taken into account for seniority-related rights.
d. During the trial period there is a duty on the part of both employer and employee 'to execute the experiences that are the subject-matter of the trial'. Nothing is said about what happens if the 'duty to try' is not actually discharged but it is clear that, when the trial period is finished, no dismissal because of the ineptitude of the employee is possible; this ineptitude could be verified through these experiences.
e. During the trial period both the employer and the employee have the right to cease the trial, seemingly without the necessity to justify their decision and with the parties having no duty to indemnify each other.
f. When the trial period is finished, the silence of the parties means that the trial period has succeeded and immediately after its end a normal labour contract will start, that will usually be interpreted as being for an indefinite period of time.
g. Situations of temporary disability, birth, adoption, custody for adoption purposes, foster family, risk during pregnancy, risk during breastfeeding, and gender violence, which affect the worker during the trial period, always interrupt the calculation that an agreement is reached between both parties.
h. The termination at the employer's request of the labour contract, during the trial period, will be void in the case of workers due to pregnancy, from the date of the start of the pregnancy until the beginning of the suspension period due to birth, unless there are reasons not related to pregnancy or motherhood.

IV. Form of the Contract

228. As to the form of the contract, the very old rule of Spanish contractual law 'if the parties wish to contract, let them contract without further ado'[4] is applied to the labour contract.

229. So, the rule is that the labour contract can be entered into in writing, or by spoken word or just by clear signs, customary or not.

230. The WSA requires, however, a written form in some cases: contracts for training, contracts for a definite period of time or for a certain and precise service or endeavour (whose duration is more than four weeks). As we have seen, most of the specific regulations of the 'special labour relationships' too (high-ranking personnel, artists, commercial travellers, etc.) require a written form. Previous laws said too from time to time that certain labour contracts should be in writing; but time after time court decisions have said either that the written form does not affect the validity or the efficacy of the contract itself, or that the mandatory written form only implies that if it does not exist, the onus of the proof of the existence of the contract lies with the party that maintains it does.

231. This doctrine about the validity of the contract when the written form does not exist is in a certain sense taken up again by the WSA: it says that in this case the contract is deemed to be concluded for an indefinite period of time, except if it is proved that the contract is of temporal nature. In other words, in the ES the onus of the proof regarding limitation of the contract lies with the employer, who is obliged to provide a written agreement.

232. The WSA also establishes that each of the parties may demand the written form, even after the labour relationship has begun.

233. Of course, as the written form is not necessary, there is no need to speak of any type of obligatory content, or mandatory clauses.

234. It should be said nevertheless that many labour contracts are made in writing, especially when the employer wants to have proof of some special clauses (for instance, if the contract has special duties for the employee). Again, in the cases of enterprises with a large or an average amount of bureaucracy, there is actually a contract in writing which takes the form of a letter or a document asking for work coming from the employee and an answer from the employer accepting him specifying, at least, the type of work and the qualifications that the employee has, and the collective agreement which is applicable.

4. The rule was first formally enacted in 1348 in the *Ordenamiento de Alcalá*, Tit. XVI, *Ley única*; today it is contained in Art. 1278 of the Civil Code: Art. 51 of the Commercial Code; and Article 8 of the WSA.

235. The employer is obliged to give to the employees' representatives in the enterprise a copy of every labour contract put in writing; this copy must contain the essential elements of the contract. The employer is also obliged to inform the employee – within two months since the beginning of the labour relationship – of his essential work conditions when the duration of the labour contract is longer than four weeks; among them being the date of the beginning of the contract, employer's address, employees' classification, amount of wages, working time, holidays, applying collective agreement. When the employee has his contract in writing and the contract contains these conditions, this employer's duty is accomplished.

V. Capacity of the Parties

236. As far as the employer is concerned, there is no special labour law capacity rule; he can be either a natural or moral person and of course he can contract in person or through his representatives. Civil, commercial or administrative rules are applied according to the nature of the employer. If he is a natural person, the normal full legal age of 18 will be required.

237. As for the employee, sex, marital status, social origin, race or other traits are not limitations on entry to a legal contract. The WSA does not contain a specific rule but implicitly states it in Article 17 which forbids – in accordance with Article 14 of the Constitution – discrimination in employment for these reasons.

238. The age of a person influences his capacity to enter into a labour contract, in accordance with the following norms:

a. Minors of 16 years cannot enter into a labour contract; if the contract is made, it is void, but the general rule of the WSA on the nullity of the contract is that the employer must pay wages as if it is a valid contract.
b. Minors under 18 years – but over 16 – need, in order to enter into a labour contract, the authorization or assistance of their father, or mother or if they have no parent, their legal guardians. But if these minors are married or, with the knowledge and consent of their parents, live independently of them, they have full legal capacity to enter into a labour contract.
c. Persons of more than 18 years of age have no legal incapacity. At present, this limit of age coincides with the normal civil age.
d. The WSA authorized the Government to establish a maximum age to be part of the labour contract as an employee, bearing in mind resources of the social security system and the situation of the labour market, which to date has not been established. The Constitutional Court declared that the termination of the labour contract for this reason 'in a direct and unconditional way' should be unconstitutional. It must be interpreted whether the termination of the labour relationship bargained individually or through collective agreement, improves the economic conditions of the employee's retirement, in which case it will not be unconstitutional. For this reason, the WSA currently establishes that collective

agreements can establish clauses for the termination of the employment contract due to compliance by the worker of an age equal to or greater than 68 years, provided that, among other requirements, said measure contributes to generational change through the indefinite contract, full-time hiring, of at least one new worker.

239. Special rules which are not actually peculiar to labour law, but are rules of civil law, apply to cases such as those of completely deaf-mutes, prodigals, or people with mental disorder. The gist of these rules, as applied to labour contracts, or to acts done in furtherance of the contract, is that they are valid if it is not satisfactorily proven that the employee was completely out of his mind when he acted, provided of course that the contract or the act is not clearly against the interests of the employee, or that some reasonable doubt arises about the employer having taken advantage of the situation.

VI. Foreign Workers

240. Although it is not actually a theme of 'capacity to work' this point is as good as any other to say a few words about foreign workers in Spain (leaving aside the subject of Spanish workers abroad which is dealt with, mainly, through a very complex net of bilateral international treaties with many countries, other than these of the EU).

241. This matter is regulated by Organic Act 4/2000 of 11 January, on Rights and Liberties of Foreign People in Spain, and Royal Decree 557/2011, of 20 April.

242. The general rule is that a foreigner is admitted to work as an employee, in Spain, depending on the national situation of employment. Admission to work is certified in a 'labour authorization' issued by the Ministry of Employment. The petitioner must prove that a labour contract or an offer to work exists.

243. The first authorization or 'initial' one is limited to a territory or to an occupation. Successive authorizations do not have these limitations. The employer is normally the solicitor, being the subject who has the initiative of contracting; the employee may also do this if he is in Spain.

244. The foreigner employee has the same rights and duties as a Spanish employee, including rights in social security and collective rights (trade union freedom, right to strike, and employees' representation in the enterprise). Discrimination from the employer because a worker is a foreigner is expressly prohibited.

245. Since Spain is a member of the European Union, the application of the free movement of workers rule is obviously made for Union citizens.

246. Exceptionally, authorization is not required for certain activities: university professors, scientific, cultural, artistic, religious, informative, cooperation with the

Spanish administration and international union representation. In these cases the acknowledgement of the Spanish authority is sufficient.

247. Since 2013, Spanish legislation has contemplated a migration channel with specific rules to attract highly qualified migrants or those with significant investment capacity – for example, for the purchase of a home starting at EUR 500,000. However, this last legal possibility is currently under review.

Chapter 2. Rights and Duties of the Parties in the Course of the Employment Relationship

§1. Introduction

248. In Spanish labour law books it is habitual not to organize the subject matter of this chapter rigidly along the lines of the duties of the employee and the duties of the employer. Rather it is considered that, as the labour relationship is bilateral and reciprocal, every duty of the employee implies a right on the side of the employer, and vice versa; in the most obvious example, wages can be considered a right to the employee (the right to receive them) or as a duty to the employer (the duty to pay them). So the tendency is to take the content of the labour contract, so to speak, and explain it as a whole, making a reference to the complex of rights and duties of the employer and employee built upon it.

249. Going back to the example, a treatment beginning with wages as a right of the employee, and followed with wages as a duty of the employer, will tend to divide a matter which can, it is thought, be studied most systematically and truly by itself. Similarly, reasoning could be made, with more or less success, with reference to almost every right and duty deriving from the labour contract.

250. An effort will be made, nevertheless, not to depart from the general outline of the editors to distinguish between the respective duties of the employee and of the employer (leaving aside, of course, matters – such as remuneration, working time, etc. – which are included in other chapters).

§2. Duties of the Employee

I. The Duty to Work

251. The first and foremost duty of the employee is the duty to work, that is, to carry out the labour which is the main object of his promise under the labour contract. A duty to work has almost no meaning if a reference is not made to the quantity and the quality of the work due.

252. As to the quantity, the amount of work due should be fixed at a point which neither allows for 'staying' at work without actually working, nor for a completely exhausting pace or rhythm of work.

253. Article 5 of the WSA includes among the 'basic duties' of the employee 'to execute the duties corresponding to the work-place, in accordance with the rules of the bona fides and diligence'. Article 20 adds:

> the employee, executing his duty to work assumed in the labour contract, must work with the diligence and collaboration that shall be determined by the law,

collective agreement, fair orders and instructions of the employer and customs. In any case, employee and employer are submitted, in their corresponding duties, to the bona fides principle.

254. These general rules should be understood with the following additions and qualifications:

- Collective bargaining agreements and even individual contracts may call for a minimum of work; the minimum so fixed comes then in lieu of custom. But it is to be understood that fixation under an individual contract cannot set an abnormally fast pace.
- There was some theoretical discussion about whether the custom concerning the amount of work due does not imply tacit agreements among the employees and so provides leeway for feather-bedding practices. But there is a consensus that the knowledge of the amount of work reasonably due actually exists and that feather-bedding is to be defined just as work below what is customary.
- In the case of urgent need in order to remedy accidents, an extraordinary or unusual amount of work can be required from the employee.
- 'Voluntary and continuous reduction of the normal or bargained (amount of) work' is a cause for just dismissal. The rule refers to normal work unless partially measured, and that again goes back to custom, by what was being usually done. The reference to the agreement between the parties about the amount of work should permit, if the pact is actually made, to specify exactly when there is fulfilment or unfulfilment of this employee's duty.

255. As to the quality of the work due, it depends upon a combination of the skills that the employee actually has and the skills for whose use he has been contracted. That having been said, the following principles will apply:

- The skills determining the type and quality of the work due are those mentioned expressly or implied by the contract; it is presumed that the employee actually has these and that the trial period has established them. It does not matter that the employee has superior skills if his contract does not ask for them. But if in practice the employer is using these superior skills these are deemed to be skills called for by the contract, no matter what the contract itself could have said.
- A skill – but more so a trade or a profession – usually implies several sub-skills which can be put to different uses; it is up to the employer to decide which of them should actually be put into effect in carrying out the labour contract unless the contract is specific about the concrete work to be performed.

256. The employee is classified within the enterprise according to his skill, and many of his conditions of work depend on his classification; his wages, to begin with, depend on his skill level, as does his opportunity for promotion. Precisely because of that the matter is prone to discussion between employer and employee. It is a type of conflict subject to judicial proceedings before the Labour Courts. There is an intimate relationship between classification and promotion, in the sense that promotion means accession to a higher or a different type of classification.

257. Article 4 WSA includes 'promotion in work' among the employee's rights. Article 24 establishes that advancements in the classification system within an enterprise must be made following the rules of the collective agreement, which will be in accordance with the professional training, merits and seniority of the employee, and also comply with the organizational rules of the employer; these rules must be common for every employee without discrimination based on sex. Likewise, Spanish labour legislation contemplates the possibility of establishing positive action measures aimed at eliminating, or compensating, situations of discrimination.

258. Collective agreements normally include some regulations on this matter and are more extensive in enterprises with high numbers of employees and different places of work. Methods of advancement through aptitude examinations, tests or training courses are probably dominant, assuming the new work place must be occupied by the most competent employee; advancement in accordance with seniority accumulated in lower classification still exists but is probably receding. The free decision of the employer is as a general rule limited to work places of special confidence or responsibility.

II. The Duty to Obey

259. The duty to obey is implied in the labour contract by its own definition; the employer has the power to give orders and the employee the duty to obey them. Article 1 WSA refers, as we have seen, to 'employees who provide their services within the domain of organization and direction of the employer'. Article 5 includes among the basic duties of the employee the duty to 'fulfil' the orders and instructions of the employer within the fair exercise of his directional powers:

- An employer's orders cannot infringe the general principle of no discrimination of an employee or a group of employees. Article 17 WSA, in fact, declares as void, among other acts, 'unilateral decisions of the employer that give rise in employment, as well as in matters of remuneration, working hours and other working conditions, to situations of direct or indirect unfavourable discrimination due to age or disability or to situations of direct or indirect discrimination due to sex, origin, including racial or ethnic origin, marital status, social condition, religion or beliefs, political ideas, sexual orientation and identity, gender expression, sexual characteristics, membership or not to unions and their agreements, kinship ties with persons belonging to or related to the company and language'. The same principle appears in Article 4 WSA as one of the employee's rights in the course of the labour relationship.
- Additionally, and deepening into the legal implications of the principle of non-discrimination, Spanish legislation (Article 17 WSA) establishes the nullity of orders to discriminate and decisions of the employer that involve unfavourable treatment of workers as a reaction to a claim made in the company or before an administrative or judicial action aimed at demanding compliance with the principle of equal treatment and non-discrimination. Likewise, it provides that failure to comply with the obligation to take protective measures against discrimination

and violence directed at LGBTI people will give rise to the assumption of responsibility by the employer in the terms established by current legislation – in this case Article 62.2 of the Law for the real and effective equality of trans people and for the guarantee of the rights of LGBTI people.

- Of course, the employer's orders cannot be vexatious or abusive even if they are externally or formally within his powers to direct; the employee has the right to be treated with the 'consideration due to his dignity' (Article 4 WSA).
- Court decisions have admitted the general presumption that any order relating to work is a proper order and shall be obeyed, although the employee can afterwards impugn them. But the presumption covers only work-connected orders, as Suarez said long ago.[5]
- So, on the contrary, non-work-connected orders are not under the legitimacy presumption and generally speaking the employee is not under a duty to obey them; even though some situations may arise, or the employee may occupy such a situation where the distinction between work and non-work is difficult to define. The duty to obey then reappears, but the employer must prove that the special circumstance exists. This problem appears especially in connection with the orders about the private life of the employee: besides the right to respect the 'employee's intimacy', included among the rights recognized by the WSA, it is clear that the employer's power to direct is outlined in the employee's duties within the strict framework of the labour relationship.

III. 'Loyalty' Duties

260. There has been some discussion in Spanish labour law on whether a special duty in respect of the loyalty of the employee exists. Today, the discussion mainly centres on what could be considered a question of 'good faith' in the performance of a contractual obligation.

261. The duty to submit to the bona fides principle on the performance of the labour contract appears repeatedly in WSA: Article 4, as one of the employee's rights; and Article 20 as a duty demanded both to the employer and to the employee.

262. Although today the discussion is put in a different way than in the past (when perhaps the parties looked for the support of a highly sophisticated historical,[6] or ideological reasoning), let us say that before the WSA some legal rules (today derogated as such but nonetheless implicitly existing in the WSA rules) are included under this general heading:

5. The duty to obey only to *quod ex officio facere tenentur*, what the trade calls for, separates the free worker from the serf, said Suarez (*De legibus ac Deo legislatore*, Book III, Ch. XXI, no. 7, Ed, Coimbra, 1612; reproduced by Instituto de Estudios Políticos, Madrid, 1967).
6. No less an authority than Otto von Gierke (*Die Wurzeln des Dienstvertrages*, in *Festschrif für Brunner*, Leipzig-Munich, 1914 Spanish translation by G. Barreiro, 'Civitas', 1982) made an all-out effort to defend the loyalty duties as based upon the old 'Germanic' ingredients of the labour contract; but that belongs to a curious 'anti-romanistic' strain of a branch of legal historians up to, and including

- the duty of secrecy;
- the duty not to accept tips, gifts or similar things which would constitute bribes, not to fulfil the labour contract, without the expressed permission of the employer. There is an exception in the cases where it is an approved custom of the trade to accept tips when the work consists of providing a service to a third person;
- the duty to advise the employer about anything lacking or defect in the materials, instruments or machines employed in the work;
- a duty to abstain from any conduct which results in prejudice to the work and damage to the work-place, materials, etc., and to work diligently to avoid such damages.

The WSA maintains explicitly the duty not to compete with the employer, which will be studied in Chapter 8.

263. An interesting perspective in relation to what a worker's duty of loyalty is has been raised by Directive (EU) 2019/1937, on the protection of persons who report breaches of Union law, and its transposition into Spanish Law – carried out in 2023 – in such a way that, from now on, in companies with fifty or more workers there is an obligation to establish an internal information system that allows workers, with legal guarantees that prevent unfavourable treatment of them, to make complaints about possible actions and omissions, in general, that may constitute infringements of European Union Law, but provided that they are within the scope of application of the acts of the European Union listed in the Annex to the aforementioned Directive, and that affect financial interests and affect the internal market. Likewise, the worker may be informed of actions or omissions that may constitute a serious or very serious criminal or administrative infraction in any administrative area – serious or very serious criminal or administrative infractions that entail an economic loss for the Public Treasury and for Social Security are expressly included.

264. The Constitutional Court has rejected the existence of a general duty of loyalty in Spanish labour law in the sense of employee's subjection to the employer's interest, which would be contrary to the constitutional system of labour relations. The Court accepts the bona fides, duty, common to every contract, which can permeate the fulfilment of employee's obligations in the case of a labour contract.

265. Perhaps it is necessary to say in this connection that the employer-employee relationship has some bearing on certain crimes. It aggravates criminal responsibility in crimes against property if the employee has taken advantage of his position; responsibility for certain misdemeanours and criminal acts will be aggravated if the guilty party is a professional, as the employee is most likely to be. And the duty on the employee derived from the labour contract to obey does not reduce, much less excuse, any crime committed.

F.W. Maitland; which, incidentally, was criticized by Max Weber as simplistic (*Wirtschaft und Gesellschaft*, 1st part, VII, 3; Spanish trans., Mexico, 1964, Vol. I, pp. 582 ff.).

§3. Duties of the Employer

266. We leave aside in this chapter those duties of the employer that are the subject-matter of Chapters 3 to 7 which of course include specific and peculiar duties of the employer. Those which will be dealt with here are, for the most part, duties which, so to speak, give the labour contract its peculiar character, or are the peculiar contractual duties of labour law.

I. Duty of Protection

267. A general duty of the employer to care for the employee is what is usually meant by the duty of protection. Being a very general heading, it is usually divided into statutory or normal duties and non-statutory, customary or informal duties.

A. Statutory Duties

268. Under statutory duties the following are to be mentioned, first of all, the duty to provide a safe place and safe conditions of work. All the extremely complex regulations of security and hygiene of work should be included here. The point is that there is, on the one hand, a statutory duty to comply with specific regulations about personal safety at work, the good condition and maintenance of machines and installations and safe 'general conditions' of the premises; and, on the other hand, there is besides a general duty implied in the labour contract which covers the possible lack of specific regulations; in this sense it is said that the employer owes, or has a duty to provide security to the employee. The WSA underlines this last point saying that 'the employee, during the performance of his services, has the right to your physical integrity and to an adequate occupational risk prevention policy'.

269. The main regulation of occupational health and safety is contained in the Labour Risks Prevention Act of 8 November 1995 (LRPA). It specifies in an extent and detailed way the employer's obligations on safety organization in the work place, namely planning of the prevention, evaluation of risks, supplying of personal protection items, etc.

270. The LRPA acknowledges the information and consultation rights of the employees' representatives on this matter; it will be dealt with in Part II, Chapter 2, §4.

271. The general rules of the LRPA are completed by a large group of executive regulations on several matters such as prevention organization in the work centre, security signalling, anti-fire and first aid facilities, health services, handling of dangerous loads, use of PC screens, etc.

272. The LRPA deals afterwards with the sanctions against the employer and worker for not observing the applicable security measures; besides the usual system of fines – and besides the fact that in certain cases non-compliance may amount to criminal tort and be prosecuted as such – there is a very peculiar and old norm (it appeared in the 1900 first Workmen's Compensation Act), which has been maintained ever since, according to which social security economic benefits to the employee, or to his dependents in case of death, will be increased – between 30% and 50% – if the accident happens to be caused by a breach of the statutory security duty. This increased indemnity amounts to awarding punitive damages which the employer cannot be insured against, insurance taken for that purpose being null and void.

273. Second, the duty to indemnify the employee for any type of expenses incurred by him in carrying out his work or, generally, his employer's orders.

274. Lastly, the duty to provide the employee with work is established by the WSA: Article 4 includes among the employee's rights during the labour relationship, the right to carry out effective work. The law has considerably reinforced this right since prior rules only required it when not providing work was due to the intention to vex the employee; or when not providing work 'considerably harmed' the professional training and development of the capacities and skills of the employee.

B. Non-statutory Protection Duties

275. In the past, some initiatives of the employer which implied benefits for the employee (for instance, all the miscellaneous benefits usually included under the rather general heading human relations: sports, recreation or artistic activities or clubs; scholarships for the employee or for members of his family; aid in nurseries; kindergartens for the employee's family, etc.) were considered deriving from the duty of protection. Today, when these benefits exist, they are established by the collective agreement.

276. If the employer voluntarily provides these types of benefits and the provision is maintained for a long period of time – the period depending on the nature of benefits – then surely, he is under a duty to continue to provide them, because most probably the benefits will be held by the courts to be an implied condition of the labour contract to which the employee is entitled. Actually, many of today's formal protection duties start as informal or non-mandatory duties met by enlightened employers and are afterwards generalized up to a point at which, either through collective bargaining (as we have said), or through legislation, they are transferred into formal or statutory protections.

277. There was support in the past for the opinion that social security contributions of the employer were part of, or derived from, his duty to protect the employee. By now, social security contributions are generally conceived as earmarked taxes on wages, or with wages as a basis for their calculation, independent of any such specific duty.

II. Ius Variandi

278. If there is a duty, as stated above, on the part of the employee to work according to his skills, there is a negative duty on the part of the employer not to give work-connected orders which will abuse the employee's duty. Work orders, except in emergencies, are limited by the work that is called for by the labour contract. Nevertheless, maintaining the above rule is usually thought to be a rather formal and unrealistic conception of the labour relationship. In fact, the skills change through the duration of the contract, especially if the contract is for a long period of time. When this happens the same initial labour contract is deemed to continue with the new, modified and usually higher skills, without any formal declaration by the parties – although of course, a formal declaration may occasionally exist – except that, if not previously granted, the employee may ask for the higher classification that the new skills he is using commands. So, more or less smoothly and unnoticed, the work situation changes from this point of view; and the method of change is the orders or proposals which, with the express or tacit assent of the employee, emanate from the employer. It is exactly this fact to which the expression ius variandi refers, which is not actually a right to change, but a right to initiate changes, assigned to the employer.

279. Of course, the employer may not introduce unilateral and substantial modifications in the labour contract. If the projected modifications refer to a 'substantial' condition of work (type of work, working time, place of work, remunerations, for instance) and touch a group of employees or all of them, it is necessary to obtain the acceptance of their representatives (work centre council or shop stewards, although the latter has preference). If the projected modification touches an employee, and he does not agree, he may claim before the Labour Court or terminate his labour relationship, in the second case he has a right to damages.

When an agreement between the parties is not possible during bona fides bargaining, the employer may unilaterally decide the modification with a later judicial control. The period of bargaining and consultation may be substituted by a mediation or arbitration proceeding agreed by the employer and employees' representatives. The law provides for some norms about this proceeding of bargaining and consultation in enterprises without a legal representation of employees: in this case, allowing the employees to appoint a special representation for this purpose, that can be assumed either by the workers themselves directly or by the most representative unions on their behalf.

III. Disciplinary Power

280. Reference was made at the beginning of this chapter to the connection between rights and duties of both parties and the difficulties in making a distinction between them. Perhaps these difficulties appear nowhere more clearly than in a treatment of the powers conferred by the law on the employer to discipline the employee when the employee's duties are not properly discharged. The disciplinary power of the employer can be studied as a corollary of his power or right to give orders, or as a consequence of the duties – to work, to obey, etc. – of the employee.

281. In any case, the employer does have disciplinary powers; limited of course, by the labour contract and by the type of sanctions that can be imposed upon the employee (another limitation is the power of the courts to review the sanctions; that will be studied in Chapter 10 of this Part I).

All this is explicitly stated in Article 58 WSA which empowers the employer to sanction the employee because of contractual breaches, according to legal and collectively bargained rules.

282. As in every disciplinary law the distinction has to be made between the types of acts and conduct that can be corrected and the types of corrections themselves.

283. As to the acts or conducts which can be punished, only a general rule can be given, namely, that any branch of the contractual duties is included. 'Contractual' is the word to be underlined, in the sense that only the duties emanating from the labour contract, or rather the failure to comply with them, can be subject to disciplinary sanction. Professional regulations frequently contain a more or less complete list of them, but they usually end with one last item which refers to any type of conduct similar or analogous to those listed. Again, normally a distinction is made within the list according to the seriousness of the failure to comply, but the seriousness depends on the particular circumstances of each case. To sum up, the criminal rule nullum crimen sine lege, to say the least, has not the precision and rigidity proper of criminal law.

284. As to the punishments, instead, the rule *nulla poena sine lege* applies strictly. The types of disciplinary measures that can be taken against the employee are very precisely written down. The most important and serious one is the dismissal of the employee, which will be studied in Chapter 6 of this Part I. Lighter sanctions include oral or written reproach; suspension of work and pay for so many days or weeks according to the seriousness of the fault; retardation of possible promotions; transfer of the workplace. At present, the WSA expressly forbids as sanction the reduction of annual vacation and fines.

The most important sanctions must be notified in writing to the employee, stating their type and the concrete act or conduct upon which they are based.

285. It should be repeated that, as will be seen, this type of decision by the employer can be reviewed, at the request of the employee, by the Labour Court. Finally, it should be added that quite a short statute of limitations applies to the use of disciplinary powers; this also will be dealt with in Chapter 10.4 of this Part. I , when addressing the limitation period to apply the disciplinary power of the employer.

IV. Duties of the Employer Towards Third Parties

286. These are, of course, duties of the employer to third parties because of the labour contract or rather because of acts of the employee in carrying out his duties under the contract.

287. Most of the subject matter under this heading belongs to either civil or criminal law. But since the matter has a close relationship with the labour contract the general principles of Spanish law concerning the matter can be briefly discussed here.

288. On civil torts, Article 1.902 of the Civil Code says that 'he who through negligent acts or omissions causes damage to others shall repair the damage caused'. And Article 1.903 follows by saying that this responsibility in tort emerges not only from our own acts but also from the acts of persons who are under our care or orders. With what now sounds like old terminology, as an example of its general rule, Article 1.903 says that 'the owners or directors of a workplace are responsible (to third parties) for the damages caused by their servants in the course, or on the occasion of, their services'. There are abundant and evolving Supreme Court decisions which increasingly tend to say that even if (i) the responsibility of the employee is based upon negligence, either through his act or omission, being (ii) the derived responsibility of the employer independent of any negligence on his part, then (iii) the employer's is an 'objectified' or in re ipsa responsibility. In more recent decisions, the jurisprudence has avoided a full objectified responsibility of the employer.

289. On criminal torts Article 116 of the Criminal Code says that every person who is responsible for the crime is also responsible for the damages it causes. Responsibility for these damages, in the case of the insolvency of the employee, passes on to the employer if, again, the crime is committed because of the employee's duties or services (according to Article 120 of the Criminal Code). Even more widely here in the Supreme Court decisions use the theory of 'objectified' or in re ipsa responsibility. Nevertheless, the decisions of the Criminal Section of the Supreme Court are highly variable in their application to the many different hypotheses of damages caused to third parties by the criminal conduct of employees in the service of the employer. Transport, construction work and banking are, among other activities, the situations in which most of the cases dealing with criminal negligence have arisen.

In 2010, the Criminal Code was amended to enter into Article 116 the criminal liability of the legal person, which is basically civil liability in certain cases.

Chapter 3. Working Time, Annual Vacation, Holidays (Including Overtime, Work on Sundays)

290. We will deal with the topics included in this chapter in the following order.

- hours of work, normal hours;
- non-periodic interruptions in the work: permits and licences;
- overtime;
- weekly rest;
- holidays;
- annual vacation;
- digital disconnection.

§1. Hours of Work, Normal Hours

291. In the past there was a tendency in Spanish law and practice to consider not the day but the week as the period over which to establish the normal working time. More recently there has been a tendency to consider the year as a reference unit to establish this time. These changes obviously allow more flexibility in the distribution of work time.

292. According to Article 34 WSA, the normal working time will be fixed by collective agreement or individual contract, and in any case will not exceed forty hours a week on a yearly average. The law permits a non-regular distribution of the daily working time provided that: (a) there is a rest period of at least twelve hours between two working days; and (b) normal hours are not more than nine hours a day unless a different working time distribution is fixed by collective bargaining. In the latter, the employer may collectively agree with his employees on the so-called compensated annual calendar perhaps allowing for some extra holidays, or taking all Saturdays off work, or providing for more days than the mandatory number for annual vacation – to give some examples – the result being a normal working day of nine hours and some minutes.

293. The 'maximum legal working week' of forty hours has a considerable number of exceptions.

294. To begin with there are, of course, many collective bargaining agreements providing for a shorter working week of thirty-five, or even fewer, hours a week. Nevertheless, we have observed for some years collective agreements with a longer working time, in order to maintain or recover levels of competition of enterprises.

295. A specific regulation is given for a partial working time contract (Article 12 WSA and additional executive rules) successively reformed in recent years. It is a type of contract whose services are for a number of hours of work in the day, the week, the month or the year lower than in a comparable contract of full-time working. It must be put in writing and specify the number of ordinary hours of work and their distribution.

296. Essential notes for this type of contract are the following:

a. Employees with a partial working time contract have the same rights as other employees, but in certain cases, rights will be recognized in a proportional measure to the time worked.
b. These employees may not work overtime, except in a limited number of cases mentioned by the law. In contrast, they may work 'complementary hours', i.e., the hours worked as additional to the ordinary hours agreed in the contract. To make it legal, an agreement between the parties in writing is necessary, celebrated at any time in the course of the labour relation. In any case, the law only allows 'complementary hours' to be carried out when the contract contemplates a working day of at least ten hours per week on an annual basis – however, in contracts with a duration of less than ten hours, the law allows a certain number of 'complementary hours' to be carried out voluntarily.
c. 'Complementary hours' may not exceed 30% of the ordinary hours of work, the collective agreement may allow up to 60%. These hours may be agreed only in a partial working time contract with an ordinary working time of not less than ten hours per week in an annual computation. They must be paid as ordinary hours and be taken into account in the contribution to social security. Although the worker may renounce this agreement, after one year of its conclusion, when has to attend to family responsibilities, registers training needs, or is incompatible with another part-time labour contract.
d. The daily work time of these employees will be recorded every day and totalized monthly. The employer must deliver, besides the receipt of wages, a summary of hours worked in the month, ordinary and complementary; he must also keep the summaries of the monthly working time for at least four years.
e. Conversion of a full-time contract into a partial working time one or vice versa will be always voluntary for the employee, never unilaterally imposed by the employer, nor either as a modality of ius variandi. The employee will not be sanctioned or penalized if he is against the conversion of the contract.
f. Employees with a partial working time contract must be informed concerning the vacant places of work in the enterprise in order to obtain the voluntary conversion of their contract into a full working time one or vice versa or to increase the hours of work of a partial working time contract. The employer must, if possible, take into consideration these requests of the employees; his refusal must be notified in writing explaining the reasons.

297. Additionally, there are some activities in which the legal maximum is less than forty hours. This is the case for works with special conditions of risk or stress, underground works in mines and public works, and activities in frost chambers. Limitations on working time for these cases are established by Royal Decree 1561/1995 of 21 September. In contrast, the Royal Decree 1561/1995 contains special provisions for other activities where the normal working day may be extended under certain circumstances and under specific conditions: porters and guards; road, railway and air transportation; merchant navy and fisheries; hotel and tourist-related industries and services; and others.

298. Examples could also be given of the so-called non-regular working time; for instance, the cases regulated by Royal Decree 1561/1995 for 'fractionated daily working time'. This refers to service activities where the work is done in a non-continuous way within a twelve-hour period. Collective bargaining will establish hours of rest between two working days. There are several other exceptions, but they are mostly connected with the allowance for overtime and they will be considered below.

299. A legal assumption with its own characteristics is the one contemplated by the WSA in relation to employees who are victims of gender violence, sexual violence, or victims of terrorism. In these cases, Spanish law recognizes these employees, among other rights, the right to reduce the working day with a proportional reduction in wage, as well as the right to reorganize working time, through the adaptation of the schedule, the application of a flexible schedule, or other forms of working time organization used in the company.

§2. Non-periodic Interruptions in the Work: Permits and Licences

300. Spanish Law contemplates in its regulations a set of cases in which justified interruption of the provision of work is possible. These are non-periodic interruptions in the provision of work that have their origin in the existence of events of a personal, family, work or even trade union nature. Although the main reference standard, in this case, the WSA (Article 37), usually classifies these interruptions as permits, today they are considered to be the rights of the worker, and not interruptions that depend in any case on the unilateral will of the employer.

301. The cases in which a worker is recognized the right to interrupt his work, without loss of remuneration, are the following:

a. Marriage of the worker or registration of the unmarried partner – fifteen days.
b. Serious accident or illness, hospitalization or surgical intervention without hospitalization that requires home rest for certain parents – five days.
c. Death of the spouse, common-law partner or certain parents – between two and four days.
d. Transfer of the habitual residence – one day.
e. Compliance with an inexcusable duty of a public and personal nature, including the exercise of active suffrage – the essential time or what is provided by the legal or conventional regulatory norm.
f. Performs functions of a trade union or worker representation nature, in the terms established by the corresponding legal or conventional standard.
g. Carrying out prenatal examinations and childbirth preparation techniques, if they must be carried out during the working time – for the necessary time.

h. Attendance at the mandatory information and preparation sessions in cases of adoption or fostering, if they must be carried out during the working time – for the necessary time.
i. Due to the impossibility of accessing the workplace or traveling through traffic routes to get there, as a consequence of the recommendations, limitations, or travel prohibitions established by the competent authorities, as well as when a situation of serious and imminent risk occurs, including those derived from a catastrophe or adverse meteorological phenomenon – up to four days, with the possibility of extension until the circumstances that justified it disappear.
j. For the time essential to carry out the preparatory acts for the donation of human organs or tissues, provided that they must take place within the work day.
k. In the cases of birth, adoption, custody for the purposes of adoption or fostering – the law recognizes the right to one hour of absence from work to care for the infant until he or she is 9 months old. However, in these cases the law also recognizes the right to opt for a reduction in working hours, half an hour a day, which could be accumulated for full days.

302. Other cases in which the Spanish law recognizes the right for the worker to obtain a licence or permit that interrupts his work are:

a. Carrying out exams and training courses (Article 23 WSA).
b. The exercise of their representative functions by elected representatives of the trade unions – although in this case it would not be paid (Article 9.1 a) Trade Union Freedom Act (TUA)).
c. The participation of the worker, as a representative of a trade union, in the negotiating committees of collective agreements (Article 9.2 TUA) – this is a paid leave.
d. If the worker is appointed president or member of a polling station, and the political election is on a working day – the leave is paid in this case and for the entire working day.
e. If the day of a political election is of a work nature, every worker may have up to four hours off to exercise the right to vote.

§3. OVERTIME

303. Any working time up to and over forty hours a week (or whatever legal or bargained lower limit exists, in accordance with what was said above) is deemed to be overtime. Two questions will be considered in relation to overtime; when, and in what amounts, it is allowed; and what are the rates of pay.

304. With reference to the first question; for 'normal' activities no more than eighty hours a year are allowed, except in most extraordinary circumstances such as clear or imminent danger because of some accident, or to resume production after it.

305. The actual time of overtime work done, needless to say, is very much related to the traditions and customs of every branch, the wage level and the situation of employment. A tendency for reduced overtime has been noticeable for some years. A certain number of collective agreements establish rules for this.

306. As to the second question, the rate of pay for overtime, Article 35 WSA states that it shall be set by collective agreement or individual contract at not less than the ordinary hourly rate if overtime is not compensated with an equivalent time of paid rest. If no agreement exists, overtime must be compensated with rest time within the following four months.

307. When a collective agreement provides for overtime payment, it is frequently separated into the type of overtime hours; whether they are the first two hours or additional hours, whether they are worked on Sundays or holidays, for example. A trend for recognizing free time instead of pay is perceptible in the most recent collective bargaining.

308. A troublesome problem has always been, and still is, the basis, or basic rate, upon which the percentage for overtime applies, due to the complexities of the basic rates that will be studied in Chapter 4 below. Let us say that, generally, remunerations are taken as a basis, but not productivity bonuses (although the employee can obtain a bonus within the overtime itself); but very frequently collective agreements avoid the problem by establishing, for every category and type of work, the rate of overtime as a fixed amount in euro.

309. The WSA specifies that 'overtime work is voluntary, unless it has bargained in a collective agreement or in the individual labour contract'; and this is under the limit per year noted above. In practice, a number of collective agreements effectively make obligatory overtime in certain circumstances justified by the enterprise's activity. Court decisions have decided in these cases over the contractual breach of the bona fides principle.

310. The law forbids overtime to certain types of employees: minors under 18 years, employees with part-time labour contracts, employees on the night shift, and handicapped employees.

§4. Weekly Rest

311. The general rule on this matter is stated in Article 37.1 WSA: 'Employees have a right to a minimum rest period, which may be accumulated each two weeks, of a day and a half without interruption, which as a general rule shall include Sunday and either the preceding Saturday afternoon or the following Monday morning.' For employees who are minors (under 18 years), the weekly rest period shall be two days.

The rule of possible accumulation of the rest in a two-week period means that in certain activities the collective agreement or the individual contract may fix a three-day uninterrupted rest every fourteen days.

312. Article 37.1 WSA authorizes the Government to establish 'a different weekly rest system' for specific activities. This has been effectively made by the Royal Decree 1561/1995 for guards, agriculture, shops and hostelry-connected activities; road, railway and air transport. In these cases, the half-day corresponding to each week may be accumulated in a four-week period. For seamen and fishery workers, the entire week's rest may be accumulated when the ship is in port, added to the annual vacation period or even partially paid as overtime.

313. A weekly rest period is obviously paid as a normal working day, provided there has been continuous work during the six preceding days; which actually means that the rest is paid in proportion to the days worked during the week.

314. The minimum rest period may be enlarged by collective agreement or individual contract; in collective bargaining, there are numerous examples of two days and even more days of weekly rest period.

315. Work done during the weekly rest days is overtime and is paid accordingly.

§5. Holidays

316. The WSA establishes a maximum of fourteen holidays per year, two of them shall be 'local' holidays. 1 January, 1 May, 12 October (National Spanish Day) and 25 December shall be in any case national holidays.

Article 37.2 WSA authorizes the Government to move holidays which fall in the middle of the week to the following Monday (except the four national holidays mentioned above). Autonomous regions may substitute some of the general holidays (again with the exception of the four above-mentioned national ones) with traditional ones in their territories.

317. All these holidays are paid at a normal rate as weekly rest. The WSA forbids the time off from being 'recuperated' on another day. Work done during the holiday is, as in the case of weekly rest, paid at not less than the ordinary hour more a 75%, unless there is a compensation rest.

318. The Ministry of Employment publishes the calendar listing holidays every year in the Boletín Oficial del Estado, including those specific to autonomous regions.

319. It should be remembered that it is quite usual for employer and employees at the plant level to conclude a so-called compensated annual calendar. This normally involves some additional holidays – the much appreciated 'bridges' – added to Sunday (for example, Monday or the working half of a Saturday). The working hours lost on those days are distributed throughout the rest of the working week, so that normal daily working hours may be nine hours or even more.

§6. Annual Vacation

320. As with other labour conditions, the minimum annual vacation has successively increased. The law and the collective agreement have jointly modified it.

321. Article 38.1 WSA states that the duration of annual vacation shall be fixed by collective agreement or individual contract. In no case shall it be less than thirty calendar days.

322. The following rules, concerning vacations, must be included here in addition to their duration:

a. Vacations are of course paid. Payments should be made at the beginning of the vacation. Collective agreements usually fix the rate of salaries corresponding to this period; average rate bonuses paid in the months preceding the vacation are normally included. Court decisions have excluded in this rate remuneration of overtime corresponding to the preceding period of holidays.
b. Vacations are mandatory in the sense that the employer and employee cannot take away the vacation by paying double wages. This is so much the case that the employee cannot apply to the Labour Court for the payment of vacations – except in the case where the labour contract is ended – but for the fixing of the days in which the vacation has to take place.
c. Usually the thirty days of vacations are continuous; but according to the ILO Convention they can be divided, provided that one of the fractions is of no less than two weeks.
d. As for the moment of the year when the vacation is taken, the WSA maintains an old rule stating that it shall be fixed by agreement between the employer and employee. If they do not agree on the exact dates, the Labour Court decides (usually basing this decision upon trade customs). Collective agreements may fix general rules on this; the vacation is usually taken during the summertime either by closing the shop during the vacation or by establishing shifts.
e. Again it is not very difficult to find trade agreements which provide for longer periods of annual vacation.

323. When the fixed period of vacation coincides with the temporal incapacity of the pregnant woman, with childbirth or with a different cause of suspension of the labour contract, the employee has the right to take a vacation at a different date, even if the year has passed. If that period coincides with another cause of temporal incapacity, the employee may take his vacation after the end of this incapacity, provided no more than eighteen months from the end of the year have passed.

§7. Digital Disconnection

324. An aspect linked to digital management that should not be ignored is the digital disconnection of workers. This disconnection has been recognized as a right in Spain and has its legal origin in Article 18.4 of the Spanish Constitution, which establishes that the law will limit the use of computer systems to guarantee the honour, and personal and family privacy of citizens, and the full exercise of their rights.

325. More specifically, Article 20 bis WSA recognizes the right of workers to digital disconnection from the use of digital devices – including video surveillance and geolocation devices. This right to disconnection has had legislative development, especially in the field of data protection regulations, such that this right is recognized within the framework of the right to privacy in the use of digital devices in the workplace. Said regulations expressly state that the right to digital disconnection aims to guarantee, outside of legally or conventionally established working time, respect for workers' rest time, permits and vacations, as well as their personal and family privacy.

326. However, it is a right whose realization must occur within the scope of dialogue and negotiation between the employer and the workers' representatives, since the current regulations establish that it is the employer, after hearing the workers' representatives, who must develop an internal policy aimed at employees, in which the modalities for exercising this right to disconnection must be defined, as well as training and awareness-raising actions for workers on the reasonable use of technological tools, for the purposes of avoiding the risk of computer fatigue.

Chapter 4. Remuneration and Benefits

327. The following scheme will be used to deal with this rather complicated part of Spanish labour law:

- definition and concepts;
- types of wages;
- minimum wages;
- wages above the minimum;
- benefits tied to wages;
- protective measures.

§1. Definition and Concepts

328. The following definition is taken from the elaborate Article 26 WSA, which repeats, essentially, preceding rules: 'Salary will be considered the totality of the economic receipts of workers, in money or in kind, for the professional provision of labor services on behalf of others, whether they reward actual work, whatever the form of remuneration, or rest periods computable as work.'

329. Of course, the employee can receive benefits from his employer due to the latter's liberality or for reasons not connected with the contract of employment; but the presumption is contrary to this. According to an old decision of the Supreme Court, 'the economic nature of the labour contract does not support the opinion that amounts paid (by the employer) to the employee are due to altruistic impulses'.

§2. Types of Wages

330. Several criteria may be used to classify the different types of wages; the facts or units used for this determination, and the form in which they are paid, being the most important.

331. Using the first of these two criteria, the distinction is made of course between time wages and piece wages; and a combination of the two systems (time wages plus some kinds of productivity bonuses).

332. As to time wages, they are deemed to be the wages fixed only in consideration of the time at work without paying attention to the work done, except that the labour contract could provide for a minimum of work.

333. Conversely piece wages are those fixed, taking care of only the amount and the quality of the work done, leaving aside the time spent (in theory, that is; in practice to fix the piece rate the normal time to do the work has to be taken into consideration).

334. Time wages are normal and standard in Spain for every type of work; pure piece rates are not; but – mainly for production work – some combination of time plus productivity bonuses is very usual, the bonus being dependent on work accomplished. The tariffs for these supplementary piece rates – this is what they are actually – can be established by the employer, consulting the employees' representatives. Where productivity bonuses are a feature of the trade, collective agreements tended to be very detailed, perhaps providing for group, besides individual bonuses.

335. No longer very common are the so-called tareas, the type of work in which the employee sets his own pace for completing the work that his labour contract calls for daily; and once the work is done he stops working until the following day.

336. With reference to the methods of pay the distinction is between money wages and wages paid in goods and services other than money.

337. As to money wages, the old rule – memories of the truck system – is still on the law books: money wages have to be paid in legal tender. The employer can pay by means of cheque or bank transfer: in these cases, he must communicate it previously to the employees' representatives. The date and place of payment will be according to the contract or the collective agreement or, at last, according to the custom.

338. Wages in goods and services other than money may be paid. Article 26 WSA establishes they may not be more than 30% of the sum of wages due. There is an almost infinite variation of this method – housing, with or without maintenance, gas, coal, any kind of free transportation being the most usual – depending on the custom in the particular branch or industry.

339. The WSA explicitly makes a distinction between a basic wage (salario base) which can be a time wage fixed by hour, by day, by month or by year, also a piece wage; and other benefits (complementos salariales) fixed by specific circumstances present in the labour relationship. This second type of wage will be considered below (§5).

§3. Minimum Wages

340. Article 27 WSA charges the Government to annually fix the inter-profession minimum wage after consultation with the most representative employers' associations and trade unions. This system was established in 1963 and has been in use since then.

The minimum wage rate applies to employees not covered by collective agreements with higher wages and also to those whose individual contracts do not establish a higher rate. There is some discussion about what percentage of the labour force works at the minimum rate; about 10% is the percentage usually given by well-known authorities; so 90% work for wages above the minimum.

341. Until 1997, the Government fixed not just one but two minimum wages: one for adult workers – older than 18 years – and another for workers from 16 to 18 years. This difference was eliminated in 1998.

342. Since 1963, the minimum wage has been: ESP 60 (1963), 84 (1966), 96 (1967), 102 (1968), 120 (1970), 136 (1971), 156 (1972), 186 (1973), 225 (1974), 280 (1975), 345 and 380 (1976), 440 and 500 (1977), 548 and 600 (1978), 640 and 692 (1979), 759 (1980), 854 (1981), 948 (1982), 1,072 (1983), 1,158 (1984), 1,239 (1985), 1,338 (1986), 1,045 (1987), 1,468 (1988), 1,556 (1989), 1,667 (1990), 1,775 (1991), 1,876 (1992), 1,951 (1993), 2,019 (1994), 2,090 (1995), 2,164 (1996), 2,221 (1997), 2,268 (1998), 2,309 (1999), 2,356 (2000), 2,404 (2001) – fixed on 'pesetas' -. Since 2002, fixed on euros: EUR 14.74 (2002), 15.04 (2003), 16.36 (2004), 17.10 (2005), 18.03 (2006), 19.02 (2007), 20 (2008), 21.11 (2010), 21.38 (2011), 21.38 (2012), 21.51 (2013), 21.51 (2014), 31.62 (2015), 21.84 (2016), 23.59 (2017), 24.53 (2018), 30.00 (2019), 31.66 (2020), 32.17 (2021), 33.33 (2022), 36 (2023), 37.80 (2024).

343. In recent years the minimum wage has registered a notable increase in its amount. More specifically, in the period 2018–2024, it has increased by 35.10%. This increase is explained by the will of the Government of Spain to comply with the provisions of Article 4 of the European Social Charter: 'All workers have the right to a fair remuneration sufficient for a decent standard of living for themselves and their families.'

344. The minimum wage is increased by the so-called mandatory benefits. These are the types of calculation usually made: to the minimum wage should be added one-sixth for Sundays, bonuses for July and December, vacations, holidays, seniority, and this will be the result. For the minimum wage of EUR 37.80 :

> 37.80 (a) + 37.80 / 6 (b) + 37.80 /10 (c) + 60 × 37.80 / 365 (d) + 30 × 37.80 / 365 (e) + 14 × 37.80 / 365 (f)
>
> The result is 58.63 euros per day for a normal working day, where (a) is the minimum; (b) is Sunday pay; (c) is seniority (an example); (d) is July and December bonuses; (e) is vacation pay; and (f) is holiday pay.

§4. Wages above the Minimum

345. In the past, wages above the minimum were established mainly through labour ordinances but now they are agreed upon through collective bargaining, most of which is actually concerned with wage rates.

346. Wage rates in collective bargaining agreements are highly diversified, of course, according to personal qualifications and type of work. And there are important differentials – even for what seem to be the same qualifications – between the different branches of industry and of the services.

347. Above the collective bargaining wages there are the wages settled by individual negotiations between employer and employee. The amount of this wage drift is not well known although it is generally understood that it exists for almost every type of labour, particularly for highly skilled manual or non-manual personnel, and personnel in supervisory positions.

348. A continuous source of litigation concerns whether these 'individual' wages may or may not be absorbed by increases in the collectively bargained, or in governmental minimum, wages; with the same problem emerging between the minimum and collectively bargained wages. The general rule – unless the contract or trade agreement has a specific clause against it – is that any previously agreed higher individual wage can be consolidated into an increase negotiated through collective bargaining, or an increase in the Government-fixed minimum wage. Collective bargaining increases may also be consolidated into minimum wage increases. The decision to consolidate belongs to the employer, who must adopt it without delay. If he does not do so, he is deemed to have renounced his right.

§5. Benefits Tied to Wages

349. As we have said, the WSA establishes the distinction between a basic wage and other benefits and says that both shall be fixed by collective agreement or individual labour contract. As for the benefits, they are classified into three categories, according to the method taken to fix them.

350. First, the 'personal' circumstances of the employee. In this group, seniority bonuses are established by collective agreement adding a percentage of the basic wage for three, five or more seniority years in the enterprise; bonuses for professional degrees held by the employee, for using one or more foreign languages.

351. Second, circumstances of the work done. Collective bargaining establishes a high variation of these benefits: bonuses for dangerous, toxic or hard work and for night-shift work (normally a percentage more than normal work); bonuses for punctuality and regularity in reporting for work; productivity bonuses (referred to above regarding piece wages); remuneration for overtime, for specific responsibility of the work done, for residence in certain places, commissions paid to some categories of workers (salesmen in particular), etc.

352. Lastly, the WSA mentions the 'results' of the enterprise; this category pertains to so-called profit-sharing. Some collective agreements establish a year bonus normally not taken out of the profits of the enterprise but paid at a fixed rate or paid if the company obtains a certain amount of profits.

353. The traditional bonuses in the months of July and December must also be mentioned, as they cannot be clearly placed in any of the three groups stated above.

The WSA makes them mandatory adding that a collective agreement shall determine their amount. The usual rate is thirty days each. A certain number of collective agreements even establish three, or more, year bonuses of this type.

354. Certain compensation paid for expenses incurred by the employee in carrying out his duties (travel expenses or daily allowances; for instance) are defined by WSA as non-salary remunerations; they are normally fixed by collective agreements.

355. Needless to say all these make the wage sheet extremely complicated. Court decisions allow for the so-called globalized or simplified wages, in lump daily or weekly sums, provided that the sum total is no less than what would result from the addition of the different bonuses due to the basic rate.

§6. Protective Measures

356. A rather complicated set of measures is established for the protection of wages. The old rules have been completed by others in recent years. An acceptable classification could be the following:

a. Protection with regard to the employer. The employer is under a legal duty to pay wages at exactly the time they are due. The WSA sets the interest for delayed payment of wages at 10%. It was a firm Court rule that the increase is only due when there is no doubt that the wages are actually due and the exact amount due is known. Of course, it may be said that all legal requirements about paying legal tender and so on are measures for the protection of wages.
b. Protection concerning the employee's creditor. The minimum wage cannot be seized to pay any debts of a worker. Wages above the minimum could be seized but according to the scales established in the Code of Civil Procedure. In case of 'alimentary debts', that is, alimony or amounts to support children or other family members, the Court will decide what amount shall be seized.
c. Protection of the wage with regard to the employer's creditors. Credit for wages are preferential credits in the case of the employer's bankruptcy. We will not enter into the nightmare of how the debts for wages compete with other employer's debts. It is enough to say that debts for wages have a preferential treatment, especially those belonging to periods immediately before the bankruptcy.
d. A 'Warranty of Wages Fund', created in 1976, guarantees the payment of wages to the employee in cases of insolvency or bankruptcy of the employer up to the four months preceding insolvency or bankruptcy. The Fund is supported by a tax on wages paid by employers, this tax is today at 0.20%.

357. Wages and salaries are submitted to the tax system according to the General Income Tax Act. The WSA forbids the employer to pay the tax on wages, making void any agreement with this purpose.

Chapter 5. Incapacity to Work and Other Causes of Suspension of the Labour Contract

§1. Introduction

358. Usually in Spanish labour law books this matter is treated under the heading 'interruptions of work', meaning situations in which the labour contract is suspended for a certain time, afterwards recovering its full effects.

359. Incapacity to work due to illness (either professional or 'common') and accidents (work-connected or not) is of course the main cause of such suspensions. But several others should be placed alongside them; childbirth for the female employee; long absence due to election or designation to public office; and, again, absence due to miscellaneous causes. All these causes of suspension of work will be taken up in the order just outlined.

§2. Illness and Accidents

360. Although there is some preferential social security protection in favour of work-connected accidents and professional illnesses the basic regulations as to their effects upon the labour contract are the same as for common illnesses and accidents.

361. To understand the situation reference should be made to the social security benefits. A subsidy of 75% or 60% of the wages (including average wages for overtime, if worked) is granted in the case of the so-called temporary incapacity for work during a period of time up to eighteen months; if this period elapses and medical recovery, with or without a permanent disability, has not occurred, a permanent disability should be declared forthwith, and of course, a permanent disability should be declared in any case at the end of the eighteen-month period just mentioned (or at any time within it in which the non-recovery is definitively established).

362. During the temporary disability the labour contract is suspended and the employee has a right, as soon as he is declared able to work again, to return to his employment.

363. If a permanent disability is declared, then a distinction should be made in relation to the degree of the disability:

– If there is a 'partial permanent disability' (the capacity for work is lost to the extent of at least 33% but the invalid is still able to work at his own trade), the employee has a right to be reinstated to his job with the corresponding adaptations of it to his new situation.

- If a more severe disability is declared ('total permanent' or 'absolute' disability), the labour contract ceases; although the employee can be rehired in accordance with the regulations established for disabled and handicapped persons (*infra*, Chapter 7, §4).

§3. Suspension due to Birth and Care of the Minor

364. A woman worker has a right to a rest period of sixteen weeks (two more weeks for each child from the second; and two additional weeks in the case the child is born with a disability) in the case of childbirth – a situation that includes childbirth and care of a child of less than twelve months – taken before and after the birth, as the woman wishes, although six of them must be immediately after the birth, and full time – at the same time, the legal norm contemplates that the biological mother can anticipate the suspension of her contract up to four weeks before the expected date of birth. During this period the labour contract is suspended and of course, the mother is subsequently reinstated in her previous employment. The period is covered by social security benefits with a subsidy of 100% of the wages. If the father is also an employee, he may take a part of the suspension period after the birth, simultaneously or successively with the mother. This same right, under the same conditions, is recognized to the parent other than the biological mother for the fulfilment of the duties of care for the minor established by Spanish legislation.

365. In the event that the child needs hospitalization after delivery, for a period greater than seven days, the suspension period will be extended by as many days as the child is hospitalized, with a maximum of thirteen additional weeks. Likewise, in the event of the death of the son or daughter, the suspension period will not be reduced, unless, once the six weeks of mandatory rest have ended, reinstatement to the job is requested.

366. A similar period of suspension of the labour contract is provided in the case of adoption of minors, legal guardianship with the purpose of fostering or adoption, for every adopter, keeper or foster: sixteen weeks for a child, two further weeks for each additional child, with similar distribution possibilities as in the case previously considered. The father and the mother may distribute the suspension period among them, although the law warns that the right in these cases is individual to the worker, so its exercise cannot be transferred to the other adopter, guardian or host. If the two adopters, guardians or foster parents who exercise this right work for the same company, it may limit the simultaneous enjoyment of the ten voluntary weeks for well-founded and objective reasons, duly justified in writing.

367. In cases of international adoption, when prior travel of the parents to the country of origin of the adoptee is necessary, the suspension period provided for each case may begin up to four weeks before the resolution constituting the adoption.

368. A special case of suspension of the labour contract during pregnancy is regulated by the law: when the work implies a risk to the safety or health of the mother and it is not possible to change her work place for another. The suspension period continues as necessary.

369. If the mother does not have the right to suspend her professional activity, for example, because she does not work, the father, if he works, has the right to suspend the labour contract for the period that would correspond to that of the mother.

370. With independence from what was said at the time, the WSA recognizes also for the male worker the right to suspend the labour contract for four weeks on the occasion of his paternity, including in this concept the assumptions of the birth of a child, adoption, and legal guardianship with purpose of fostering or adoption. As in the case of a woman worker, this period of suspension is expandable if the number of children is greater than one.

371. Additionally, the WSA recognizes every employee, whether man or woman, the right to parental leave, which implies the suspension of the labour contract, to care for a son, daughter or minor taken in for a period of more than one year, until now in which said minor turns eight years old. This permit, lasting no more than eight weeks, can be enjoyed continuously or discontinuously, and full-time or part-time. Although the law recognizes the employee's right to specify the start and end date of the enjoyment of this leave, the legal norm also recognizes the company's ability to decide to postpone the granting of said leave, for a reasonable period, and offering a flexible alternative, in the event that the exercise of this right has been requested by two or more employees, and the request seriously alters the correct functioning of the company.

372. A significant novelty of the current regulation, incorporated in recent years, is that the Spanish law makes it explicit that the term biological mother, for the purposes of this regulation, also includes pregnant transsexual people. Additionally, keep in mind that the differentiated treatment of maternity and paternity leave has also disappeared – from now on, and as this section indicates, the law refers to 'permit for birth and care of a minor' – with the intention of equalizing the right to parents.

§4. Military Service

373. The suspension of the labour contract in the case of compulsory military service for its full duration was considered at the time cause for suspension of the labour contract. Of course, the basic right of the employee is to be reinstated after service.

374. In 1999, the Armed Forces Act eliminated compulsory military service. However, today, the current version of the WSA does not include, among the causes of suspension of the labour contract, military service – it is the same with substitutive social service.

§5. Social Service

375. The WSA makes 'substitutive social service' equal to military service; the former is established in the Constitution for 'conscientious objectors'. The labour contract is also suspended in this case with a right to reinstatement after service and the employee must ask for reinstatement under the same terms.

376. Like military service, substitutive social service was also eliminated by the 1999 Act. Therefore, today it is not considered a cause for suspension of the labour contract.

§6. Public and Union Offices

377. The employee who is designated or elected to a public office – includes the assumption of exercise of trade union functions at a provincial or higher level – where the discharge of those duties is not compatible with those of employment, has a right to have his labour contract suspended for the period of his tenure.

The employee has also in this case a right to be reinstated and to add this period to his seniority in the enterprise.

The reinstatement must be asked for within thirty days after the end of the term of office.

378. The employee who holds a union office at a provincial or higher level has the same right. The right to be reinstated in the previous employment and the duty to ask for reinstatement within thirty days after the conclusion of the office applies also in this case.

§7. Miscellaneous Causes

379. It was very usual for old labour ordinances and now for collective bargaining agreements to provide for periods of suspension in cases such as studies, family difficulties, and some other reasonable causes, if requested by employees with a certain seniority, provided that employees in such situations do not exceed a certain percentage of the employees of the enterprise.

380. At present the WSA standardizes this right: an employee, with no less than one year of seniority, may ask for a period of suspension of the labour contract of no less than two years and up to five years. If the employee has had a period of suspension he has no right to be granted a new one, unless he has worked for at least four years in the interval.

381. In general, only cases of forced suspension of the labour contract – normally related to the election or appointment of the employee for a public office that makes it impossible to attend work – give the right to keep the job and to calculate the seniority in the company. On the contrary, if the suspension has a voluntary origin, the right that the legislation recognizes is a preferential right to re-employment in vacant positions of the same or similar category to that which the employee had, in such a way that if the job does not exist, upon request for reinstatement, the employment relationship will be terminated.

382. Among the 'miscellaneous causes' established by the WSA the following are included:

- In the case of the birth of a child, the father or mother has a right to suspend the contract starting from the birthday, to take care of the child. The maximum duration of this suspension is three years; during the first year the employee has the right to reinstatement; if the suspension continues the employee has this right only when there is a vacancy of the same or similar classification. If a new birth occurs within the period of the previous suspension period this one continues and is not accumulated with a new one. All these rules also apply in the case of legal adoption of a child.
- Employees will also have the right to a period of suspension to care for a spouse or unmarried partner, or a family member up to the second degree of consanguinity and by affinity, including the blood relative of the de facto partner, who for reasons of age, accident, illness or disability cannot take care of himself, and does not carry out paid activity. The basic regime in this case is the following:
  a. The suspension of the labour contract may not exceed two years unless a longer duration is established by collective bargaining. However, if two or more employees of the same company generate this right for the same cause, the company may limit its simultaneous exercise for well-founded and duly motivated operational reasons, and in such case, the company must offer an alternative plan that ensures the enjoyment of both employees, and that makes possible the exercise of conciliation rights.
  b. The period in which the employee remains on leave will be counted for seniority purposes, and will also have the right to attend professional training courses, to which he or she must be invited by the company. During the first year, you will have the right to reserve your job – this reservation will be extended up to eighteen months if the family is considered large. After this period, the reservation will refer to a job in the same professional group or equivalent category.
- Because of the economic, technological, organizational or production situation of the enterprise, or derived from force majeure, some or all labour contracts may be suspended. The employer must follow the proceedings established by the WSA for dismissals based on these reasons, which will be discussed below

(Chapter 6, §1.II). In this case, the employee has the right to return to his job when the aforementioned suspension ends.

- Imprisonment of the employee. The labour contract is suspended while a condemnatory sentence is passed. If the sentence is imprisonment, it is clear that the suspension continues, and the employer can decide whether to dismiss the employee or to sanction him in certain cases of crime.
- A female victim of gender violence or sexual violence, obliged to leave her workplace, has a right to suspend the contract for a maximum of six months. The judge may extend this suspension up to eighteen months. In this case, the employee has the right to return to his job when the aforementioned suspension ends.
- Of course, the labour contract is suspended in cases of strike and lock-out, as we shall see below (Part II, Chapter 4).

383. Perhaps a general comment could be made about all these situations in relation to the possibility of their long duration, especially in cases of prolonged illness. The employer can employ another employee as a substitute, in which case the condition can be attached to his labour contract that he will be dismissed when the old employee comes back.

Of course, the employer may employ another person through a temporary work firm (except in the case of a strike).

Chapter 6. Job Security

384. By way of introduction two preliminary observations should be made before discussing all the problems involved under the general heading of job security.

385. The first refers to the arrangements of the subject-matter, in order to obtain a clear picture of Spanish labour law. Lifetime employment having been dealt with in Chapter 1, §2, and seniority permeating, as will be seen, the whole subject, the termination of the employment relationship emerges as the central issue of this chapter.

386. Taking 'termination' as a very general legal term which includes the definitive ending of the labour relationship for whatever possible causes, we will distinguish between:

a. termination due to the unilateral will and decision of the employer;
b. termination due to the unilateral will and decision of the employee;
c. termination due to an agreement between employer and employee;
d. termination due to what we may provisionally call 'miscellaneous causes' (further divisions within this item will be made afterwards);
e. cases in which the labour contract is not terminated although the external appearance, so to speak, seems to call for this solution;
f. the effects of termination.

387. At present the legal situation is clarified since the WSA systematically regulates the entire topic of the termination of the labour contract.

§1. Termination due to the Unilateral Will and Decision of the Employer

388. The termination of the labour contract because of the unilateral will and decision of the employer has in Spanish labour law the name of 'despido'; the expression has no literal translation in English. 'Dismissal' is the nearest English word for it and so it will be used from now on.

389. There is a tendency to complete the definition of dismissal by adding to it the motives or causes upon which the employer's decision ought to or must be founded. This temptation should be avoided because the first and foremost problem of the law of dismissal is exactly this: does the employer actually need a cause or motive to discuss (meaning that a legally relevant cause or motive, because, as a rational being, a psychological motive, so to speak, will always be present)?

390. The answer to this question is a plain yes; except in the case of dismissals before the end of the trial period (above, Chapter 1) the employer must be prepared, if the propriety of his decision to dismiss is questioned, to offer and duly prove a legally acceptable cause for the dismissal, the consequences of not so doing being, as it will be seen, the order to reinstate or pay damages to the dismissed employee.

391. If every dismissal is to be justified as to its cause, we can follow up the discussion about dismissals distinguishing between the different legally accepted causes. Three categories of dismissal then appear:

a. disciplinary dismissals;
b. dismissals due to force majeure or technological causes;
c. dismissals due to 'objective causes'.

I. Disciplinary Dismissals

392. The cause of the dismissal which typifies disciplinary dismissals can be roughly described as a previous non-compliance or breach by the employee of his duties under the labour contract.

A. *The Causes of Disciplinary Dismissals*

393. The only breach of the contract by the employee which justifies dismissal is one which is both serious and implies the culpability of the employee, as Article 54 of the WSA says. Besides this general factor, the law adds that the following types of behaviour of the employee are causes for dismissal; repeated absences or lack of productivity; indiscipline or disobedience; insults to or mistreatment of the employer or fellow employees; breaking of bona fides or fraud; continuous default on the amount of work done; habitual drunkenness or drug addiction.

394. Some of the listed causes are widely worded to provide the remedy of dismissal because of a serious and culpable breach even if the cause is not expressly provided in Article 54 of the WSA (indiscipline, disobedience or breach of the bona fides being the most significant). The courts have had no difficulty in including a serious breach in one of the listed causes.

395. Article 54 WSA (previously, other rules that established similar lists of causes of disciplinary dismissal) is one of the rules of Spanish labour law – or of Spanish law generally – most constantly subject to scrutiny by the Labour, and Supreme Courts. An enormous mass of decisions have interpreted and applied it, always insisting on the seriousness and the deliberation of the breach; to be judged, in addition, according to the peculiar circumstances of the case (and to other circumstances; for instance: what amounts to a grievous insult depends on the regional and trade use of the vocabulary).

396. Dismissals related to collective conflicts and illegal strikes are more aptly treated in connection with them; so, we delay their study to Part II, Chapter 4.

B. The Form of Disciplinary Dismissal

397. This is a very important topic since a disciplinary dismissal is in part a formal act. The dismissal requires both (a) a formal declaration by the employer, to the employee, of his decision to dismiss, and (b) conduct by the employer in accordance with his declared decision.

398. As to (a), a letter of dismissal should be addressed by the employer to the employee stating the cause of the dismissal and the date on which it will be effective. The cause shall be stated in terms and language clear enough for the employee to have exact knowledge of the employer's reasons to dismiss; the discussion before the Labour Court, if the dismissal is taken before it, shall be centred only upon this fact and the employer will not be allowed at this stage to present others. Dismissals 'without letter' must be declared as unjustified.

399. As to (b), the employer shall unequivocally demonstrate that he abides by his own decision from the date given in the letter, not admitting any further work from the employee, and not indulging in any conduct – paying wages, for instance – which can be construed a continuation of the contract on his part.

400. Needless to say, the employer can condone the breaches of his duties by the employee; to dismiss for breach of the contract is, so to speak, a right and not a duty for him; but, in general, he shall make up his mind and dismiss no later than sixty days after knowing about the breach (and in any case not later than six months after the breach itself).

II. Dismissals due to Force Majeure or Economics or Technological Causes

401. Force majeure is to be understood in the usual Civil Law sense of 'act of God'; i.e., some extraordinary occurrence which definitely and definitively impedes the carrying out of a contract, such as fire, floods, earthquakes, explosion, war, riot, 'or a similar extraordinary occurrence not anticipated by the parties, or anticipated but inevitable'.

402. Actually, it is not the type of occurrence which gives the cause to terminate the contract but the fact that it makes definitely impossible its compliance. If the labour contract is for an indefinite period of time, the effects of the cause must be indefinite; if the labour contract is for a definite period of time the duration of the effects should be long enough to frustrate the reasonable period of compliance.

403. 'Economic or technological causes' refer to a 'situation of crisis' in which the employer cannot carry out his business for a reasonable time with reasonable profits or, rather, he has to carry it out, if at all, incurring continuous losses. Some of these circumstances are close to force majeure; some are not, in the sense that a more able, intelligent, energetic, or decisive employer could have avoided the situation. With a bit of black humour it is said that there are two types of crisis: the real ones, and the ones to sell land with a profit; leaving this aside, since there is an element in these causes which transcends the simple will of the employer, they are usually referred to in toto as force majeure 'improper'.

404. Both types of causes justify the termination of the labour contract due to the decision of the employer; it is not necessary to obtain the authorization of administrative organs as was the case until the 2012 legal reform.

405. When the case is one of force majeure 'improper' cause, the WSA establishes, initially, before the proceedings, a period of 'debate and consultation' with the employee's representatives over no more than thirty days – fifteen days in the case of companies with less than fifty employees; the period can end with an agreement between these and the employer. The agreement can include dismissals, suspensions of the labour contracts and fixing the amount of damages, among other solutions – e.g., more recently the Spanish law has regulated the reduction of employees' working hours as a measure that could be adopted in these cases. If an agreement is not reached, the proceedings before the administration continue.

406. If not all the employees are laid off, because there is only a partial closure, the order of inverse seniority, by skills, is followed in proceeding with the dismissals; but there are exceptions in favour of shop stewards and members of the work centre council, to whom is granted a priority to stay in the enterprise; of course, in proceeding to dismissals, the employer cannot discriminate.

407. Administrative or other decisions about these collective dismissals may be appealed before the Labour Court.

III. Dismissals due to Objective Causes

408. This type of dismissal has a cause that is different from the other types. This cause is by no means unitary. In a general way, we can say that it is an event that presents two traits: an event not implying the culpability of the employee and implying the breach of the internal balance of the contract, causing the employer to terminate it.

409. The WSA establishes four causes for this type of dismissal: the ineptitude of the employee, known by the employer or occurred after his employment; the lack of adaptability of the employee to the technological modification of his workplace; economic or technological causes when the number of employees effected is less than 10 in enterprises which employ fewer than 100, 10% in enterprises with between 100 and 300 employees, or 30 employees in enterprises which employ 300 or more. In the last case, it is clear that, when the number of employees affected by the decision of the employer is higher, he must follow the proceedings discussed above (II); and in the case of indefinite labour contracts concluded directly by non-profit entities for the execution of specific public plans and programs, without a stable financial endowment and financed by the Public Administrations, when there is not sufficient financing to maintain the labour contract – if the labour contract affects a number of employees greater than that reflected in the previous cause, also in this case the procedure referred to in section II must be followed.

410. This type of dismissal also requires a 'letter of dismissal' sent to the employee, as well as an advance notice of the dismissal of fifteen days. The employer is also obliged to offer to the employee a payment of damages of twenty days salary for each year of seniority in the enterprise with a maximum of a year's salary.

411. The employee has the right to six free and remunerated hours of work per week in order to facilitate the search for new employment.

412. After the decision of the employer, the employee can complain to the Labour Court, 'as if it had been a disciplinary dismissal' according to the WSA.

§2. Termination due to the Unilateral Will and Decision of the Employee

413. There is no simple accepted word or expression to cover this type of termination of the labour contract; several have been advanced, and none generally accepted; so the rather long and discursive expression 'termination due to the decision of the employee' has been legally used, the ES using at present the expression 'dimisión' (literally, resignation) of the employee. As to the popular worker's terminology, special verbal forms of 'to dismiss' are used; we hope the following translation into English is not confusing: 'I have been dismissed' ('he sido despedido') means that the worker has been fired by the employer: 'I have dismissed myself' ('me he despedido') means that the worker has terminated the contract by his own will. Don Quixote used this terminology in his relationship with Sancho Panza; although it is well known, Sancho never dismissed himself nor was dismissed by Don Quixote.

414. Of course, the general rule of law is that since nobody can be forced to work for another against his will, the employee can rescind and terminate his labour contract whenever he wishes, no matter what the duration of the labour contract is, whether it is for a definite or an indefinite period of time.

415. The WSA admits today, besides the cases of termination for just cause, others without cause or ad nutum; in the last case the employee must notify his decision to the employer within a term ('preaviso').

416. As to the cases with a just cause, the WSA says that the labour contract ends 'due to the will of the employee based on a breach of the contract by the employer'. As just causes the law includes the following: substantial modifications of the conditions of work that could harm the professional training or the dignity of the employee; or the repeated lack or delay in the payment of wages. It is an open list since the law adds any serious breach of the 'employer's duties'.

417. In any case, a peculiar case, where it must be considered that there is a just cause, although not related to what can be considered a breach of contract by the employer, is the one that contemplates the termination of the employment contract by decision of the female employee 'who is forced to permanently leave her job as a result of being a victim of gender violence or sexual violence'.

418. As to the cases of termination without just cause, the WSA does not contain a term for announcing the employee's will to terminate the contract: it must be established in collective agreements or resolved according to local custom. Nor does the WSA contain rules about the form of this announcement which can be oral or in writing, provided the employee takes reasonable means to inform the employer.

419. A last means of termination of the contract due to the unilateral will of the employee is 'quitting the job', when he leaves his work without an expressed declaration in this sense, but always with an unequivocal will to end the labour relationship. Besides its nature as an act of termination, it is also a breach of the contract which produces a right to damages for the employer.

420. Precisely because of what has been said, there is a long series of court decisions which set down the principles of this part of the law; among the most important and general ones the following should be named:

- A simple absence from work even if prolonged for several days is not to be construed as a termination of the contract by the employee. But if the absence is not justified and of a long duration, perhaps accompanied by concomitant facts from which the will to cease work on the part of the employee can be construed, it will be so construed.
- If by explicit or implicit conduct the employee has terminated the contract the employer need only take notice of it, without any further action on his part.
- If explicit, the will to terminate expressed in a certain moment may be taken by the employer at its face value; meaning that a subsequent retraction by the employee does not resurrect a contract already terminated.
- Mere disobedience of an order, even accompanied by leaving the workplace, in itself is not a termination of the contract; but disobedience accompanied by the expression or conduct which reveals at that moment a will to terminate, will be deemed to be a termination.

§3. Termination due to an Agreement Between the Employer and the Employee

421. An important and sharp distinction will be introduced at the very beginning of this topic depending on whether the agreement to be terminated was part and parcel of the labour contract itself, or was an agreement reached afterwards.

I. Agreement to Terminate Included in the Labour Contract

422. An agreement to terminate the contract at a certain date, or after the conclusion of some work, is actually what defines a labour contract for a definite period of time.

423. As we have seen above (Chapter 1, §2.I) the parties may limit the duration of the contract if some objective factor or element is present, favourable to this limitation. The contract is terminated upon the arrival of the appointed time or the conclusion of the work; but the employer (or the employee) must announce his will to stand by the agreement, because if not, and if the execution of the contract continues in fact, the labour contract will be deemed to have been renewed, and renewed for an indefinite period of time.

424. We must answer the question of whether a contract for a fixed period of time could be followed by another, or by a series, again all for fixed periods, and if the employer may rescind and terminate the relationship at the end of one of them. This is not legally possible, a prorogation for a definite period of time is only legal when the service is temporal; it is an abusive agreement, therefore null: it is assumed that the employer is attempting to retain the option to dismiss without just cause.

425. A condition can be added to the contract providing for its termination in the event of some future occurrence (for instance, the reporting back to work after a period of suspension of an employee whose position is occupied by another). The law allows for such conditions, provided that they have been provided for in advance. Again, the employer must express clearly his will to terminate when the condition occurs.

II. Agreement to Terminate During the Life of the Contract

426. Of course, an agreement to terminate a contract for a definite or indefinite period of time can be reached by the employer and the employee at any time. The labour contract will be terminated on the date and with the effects agreed upon by both parties. Most probably the parties, perhaps at the employer's insistence, will state in writing that there was, in fact, an agreement to terminate.

427. The WSA includes this type of agreement among the normal causes of termination of the contract. No other rule is added, but of course, the actual will of the two parties must be required; and at the same time, no renunciation of any employee's right may be allowed.

§4. Termination due to Miscellaneous Causes

428. These include:

a. Death of the employee. With some caution Spanish civil law admits a contract for the benefit of a third party; a promise made by the employer to the employee to hire, for instance, the son of the deceased employee in itself will not be invalid, but this promise is not a labour contract, but a promise to execute a future contract; which incidentally cannot be forced upon the employer although perhaps he can be liable to pay damages for the breach of the promise, in accordance with civil law rules.
b. Death of the employer if he is a physical person and has no heir to continue the business after his death. If the heir continues the business of the deceased, he will be deemed to be the new employer, and the previous labour contract will continue with him without any change (except for the probable right of the employee to terminate in these circumstances). Disability of the employer to continue the business and his retirement, when he works personally in the enterprise, has the same effects.
c. The legal disappearance of the employer if it is a legal person. The situation will be treated as that of dismissals due to force majeure.

§5. Cases in Which the Labour Contract Is Not Terminated

429. Consolidating rules of the same content in former laws, the WSA says that a change in the ownership or title by virtue of which the employer has his business shall not terminate the labour relationship. The labour contract or contracts will be assigned to the new owner, who becomes the new employer through the assignment and the employees will be deemed to be his employees without any change in their situation either in duties and rights or in seniority. The legal rule is, then, that agreements as to the ownership of the business are, as far as the employees are concerned, res inter allios acta – except probably for their own right under the general law of assignment for the rescinding of the contract. A business, for the purpose of this rule, is either the whole enterprise or a part of one enterprise providing it can be considered an autonomous production unit.

430. But if the new employer wants to change his business or close it, or whatever, and the effect of this can be the dismissal of the employees, the law treats the situation as dismissals that can only be justified for technological reasons.

431. There are some complex rules about the responsibilities of the previous and subsequent employer in the case of the transfer of the business, the most general rule being that both employers are responsible for amounts due to the employees, before or after the transfer, for the duration of a three-year period after it; when this time has elapsed, the responsibility belongs entirely to the new employer. Even more complex rules apply to responsibilities, in relation to social security contributions.

432. Employer and employee can agree in the labour contract that the transfer of the business will be an agreed condition for termination by the new or the old employer, and the law will allow it if it is not an abusive condition. It is generally deemed to be an abusive condition if its only intent is just to abrogate the rule that the labour contract continues after the transmission. What is meant, actually, is that the possibility of termination because of the transfer of ownership should be based upon a reasonable, but not very easily conceived, objective and justified fact or set of facts.

§6. Effects of Termination of the Contract

433. Of course the most important effect of the termination of the labour contract is the end of the relationship and the disappearance of the net of rights and duties of which it consists. Except in certain cases in which reinstatement can be ordered, there will be no continuation of the contract, although needless to say employer and employee can start a new relationship through a new labour contract.

434. The responsibilities of the parties towards each other are also the effects of the termination in certain cases. These responsibilities usually consist of damages, but there are other possibilities depending on whom is responsible for the termination, the employee or the employer. The distinction should be made, then, between rights accruing to the employee or the employer, with further distinctions according to the nature of such rights, which in turn may depend on the factual or alleged reasons brought out by the parties as the cause of the termination of the contract itself.

I. Rights of the Employee

435. Since, with reference to the employee, in some cases reinstatement and back-pay are possible, as clearly different from damages, and as there are very special types of damages, the subject will be treated under the three following headings:

a. reinstatement;
b. damages;
c. back-pay.

A. *Reinstatement*

436. Reinstatement is mandatory when the employee is a representative of the personnel in the enterprise, the Labour Court declares the dismissal as unjustified and the employee specifically chooses reinstatement instead of receiving damages for the termination of the contract.

437. In this case, if the employee is dismissed and it is proved to the satisfaction of the Labour Court that the dismissal was unjustified, the Court will order the reinstatement of the employee with back-pay. Here we come across the so-called impossibility of specific performance of a labour contract against the employer's will if he decides not to reinstate. The employer's position will be treated as a contempt of Court, and he will be ordered to pay wages, and social security contributions indefinitely, until he does reinstate, or until he reaches an agreement with the employee as to the amount of wages in lieu of reinstatement.

438. In other cases of unjustified dismissal, the employer has the right to choose between the reinstatement of the employee or the payment of damages and back pay.

439. Reinstatement is also decided when the Labour Court declares the dismissal as null and void because of discrimination or violation of the employee's fundamental rights. In any case, the WSA specifically considers null and void the dismissal of: the employee during periods of suspension of the labour contract due to birth, adoption, custody for adoption purposes, foster care, risk during pregnancy, risk during breastfeeding, enjoyment parental leave; that of pregnant employees, from the date of pregnancy to the beginning of the suspension period to which they are entitled by law; that of employees who have requested one of the non-periodic permits provided for in Article 37 WSA, or are taking them, or have requested or are taking a voluntarily requested leave of absence; employees who are victims of gender violence or sexual violence, for the exercise of their right to effective judicial protection or the rights recognized in this law to make effective their protection or their right to comprehensive social assistance; or that of employees after having returned to work at the end of the periods of suspension of the contract due to birth, adoption, custody for the purposes of adoption or foster care, provided that no more than twelve months have elapsed from the date of birth, adoption, custody for the purposes of adoption or fostering.

B. Damages

440. Damages are awarded in different cases, in different amounts; usually, they are compensatory in their nature, but sometimes, a punitive tinge will appear in the award.

If the employee has been dismissed for disciplinary reasons and the dismissal has been thrown out by the Labour Court for lack of a legal cause; the law offers to the employer a right of option: reinstatement of the employee or payment of damages (except in the case seen above of the employee representative of the personnel, in which the right to the option belongs to the employee). Damages awarded are thirty-three days' wages for each year of seniority in the enterprise, but no more than twenty-four months' wages in all.

441. When the labour contract terminates because of a decision of the employee based on a breach by the employer (modifications of the work conditions, delay or lack of payment of wages, etc., as we have seen above) the employee has a right to damages as in the case of unjustified dismissal.

442. If the employee is laid off because of force majeure or technological or economic causes he has a right to damages of twenty days' wages for each year of seniority in the enterprise up to one year's wages; provided there is no agreement between the employer and employee settling the matter for more (which frequently happens, as part of the negotiation before the closure of the plant). The 'Warranty of Wages Fund', in the cases of bankruptcy or insolvency of the employer pays damages to the employees and puts itself in the place of the employees in order to recuperate the paid amount when it becomes possible because of modification of the employer's economic situation.

The whole subject could have been provided for in a collective bargaining agreement, which will be applied if the benefits are higher.

443. Reference was made above to dismissals due to 'objective causes' (in Chapter, §1.III). First of all, the employee has a right of fifteen days' prior notice of his dismissal; if the employer does not comply with the prior notice period, he must compensate the employee with the wage corresponding to the days of notice not respected. In addition, and completely independent of this, the employee has a right to twenty days' wages for each year of seniority up to one year's wages.

II. Rights of the Employer

444. There is no question about the law forcing the employee to perform a labour contract against his will; specific performance is in this case absolutely forbidden no matter how abusive was the decision of the employee to rescind the contract. Thus we have to deal only with the possibility of damages due to the employer by the employee.

445. If the contract is for an indefinite period of time and the employee gives notice of his will to terminate within the prior notice's term (*see* above, in Chapter, §3) no damages are due; nor are they due even if the contract is for a definite period of time and a notice which is deemed to be reasonable is given.

446. Damages are due, then, when no advanced notice is given and the decision of the employee to terminate is not justified. The law does not provide for either maximum or minimum limits to these damages; the ex-employee will be obliged to pay any damages caused to the employer by his untimely and unjustified termination.

447. Perhaps some additional observations can be made in this part:

- The employer, like any bona fide creditor, is under a duty to try to reduce the damages caused by the conduct of the debtor; on this occasion, he must try to find a substitute for the employee, and must prove to the satisfaction of the court that he so tried.
- There has been some discussion about whether a clause in the labour contract providing for payment of damages to the employer by the employee in the case

of unjustified termination was or was not against public policy. The ES says that the employee who has received professional training charged to the employer for a specific service may agree with the employer to stay in the enterprise for a period of up to two years. The employee is obliged to pay damages to the employer if he terminates the labour relationship before this term ends.

III. Special Protection for Employees' Delegates or Members of Works Councils

448. Some reference has already been made to this subject, which can be completed or reiterated as follows. This special protection is accorded to 'personnel representatives', shop stewards and members of the work centre councils (we shall study this matter below in Part II, Chapter 2). The special protection consists of, namely:

- the dismissal requires a special proceeding, hearing the employee himself and the other representatives of the personnel;
- the employee cannot be dismissed during his period of office (nor up to one year after its end) because of his being a representative of the personnel or because of his legal activity as such;
- when the Labour Court finds the dismissal unjustified, the employee can choose between reinstatement and damages, contrary to the general rule, in which this choice belongs to the employer.

449. In case of partial lay-offs due to force majeure, or economic or technological reasons, the representatives will be the last to be dismissed within the category or type of work.

Chapter 7. Protection of Certain Categories of Workers and Protection Against Discrimination in Employment

450. It will be remembered that in Chapter 1 a study was made of the capacity of the parties to enter into a labour contract, with reference especially to minors; some comments were made, too, about employment of foreign workers in Spain. In taking up the subject again from a new point of view, matters of capacity will be left aside, and we will concentrate upon the conditions of the labour contract itself, as entered into by someone who has a legal capacity to contract his labour contract but whose labour conditions are subject to special rules.

451. Young workers and female workers will be treated first. Special labour contracts, like institutions related to work training which mostly refer to young persons, will be studied afterwards. A brief examination of special provisions for the handicapped will also be made. Emigration will also be dealt with briefly. The chapter will end, as its title says, with measures of protection against discrimination in employment.

§1. Young Workers

452. A minor or young worker, from the point of view of labour law, is any employee under 18 but above, of course, the age of capacity to enter a work contract. There are several prohibitions for young workers, mainly:

- works declared by the Government, after consultation with the most representative employers' associations and trade unions, as unhealthy, arduous, harmful or dangerous;
- night-shift work is also forbidden: legally 'night' is the period of time between 22.00 in the evening and 06.00 in the morning of the following day.

453. The maximum daily working time is eight hours of effective work, including training time when it exists; in cases of uninterrupted daily working time of more than four hours and a half, a rest period of at least thirty minutes is mandatory. Overtime work is absolutely forbidden.

454. In collective agreements it was not unusual to find some customary rules of the trade for the work of minors, but the amelioration of working conditions generally for adults has tended to diminish the number and relevance of those rules.

455. As we will see later, special types of contracts have been created to guarantee work training for young workers.

§2. Female Workers

456. Elsewhere reference has been made to some peculiarities of the labour contract when the employee is a woman. Some repetition will be unavoidable in discussing the subject again.

457. In any case, keep in mind from the beginning that the protection of female employees, as well as of employees who are part of the LGBTQ+ group, the latter group to which we will refer below in §6, has been the subject of significant legislative treatment in these years, on the occasion of the relevant political and legislative action deployed to achieve effective equality between all people in Spain.

458. In this sense, and first of all, we must take into account that Article 17 WSA establishes that 'shall be deemed null and void the regulatory precepts, the clauses of the collective agreements, the individual agreements and the unilateral decisions of the employer that give rise to in employment, as well as in matters of remuneration, working hours and other working conditions, to situations of direct or indirect unfavorable discrimination due to age or disability or to situations of direct or indirect discrimination due to sex, origin, including race or ethnicity, marital status, social condition, religion or convictions, political ideas, sexual orientation and identity, gender expression, sexual characteristics, membership or not to unions and their agreements, kinship ties with people belonging to or related to the company and language within of the Spanish State'.

459. Since the rules against discrimination in female employment will be discussed later in §7 of this chapter, leaving them aside for the moment, the following positive rules should be mentioned about women's work:

- the right to rest for a period of sixteen weeks in case of childbirth, distributed before and after the birth as the woman herself wishes;
- the right of a woman who has a child of breast-feeding age to have one paid hour a day, which can be divided into two half-hour periods, to care for her child; the woman can select the time, advising the employer about the period chosen; likewise, the right to accumulate the aforementioned breastfeeding hours for full days is also recognized;
- the right to a suspension of her labour contract, up to three years, to take care of a child, starting from the birthday; as we have seen above, today this is not an exclusive right of the woman, a male worker may also suspend his contract in this case.

§3. Institutions Related to Work Training

460. Apprenticeship has been long regulated in Spanish labour law. However, recently the regulations governing the insertion of young people into the labour market, and the improvement of their learning stage, have been subject to an important modification that basically aims to increase the use of the two types of labour contracts where young people are the protagonists, as well as providing greater rationality to its legal regime. Today, the law refers to it with the name of 'contract for work-linked training' ('contrato de formación en alternancia'); its rules are in Article 11.2 of the WSA and in Royal Decree 1529/2012, of 8 November – also in Royal Decree 488/1998, of 27 March. This is not the place to enter into a learned discussion of the highly technical question that such a type of contract implies, beginning with the question of whether it is a labour contract at all. The compatibility of paid work activity with the corresponding training processes in the field of vocational training, university studies or the set of training specialities recognized by the Spanish National Employment System. That circumstance tends at the very least to make it into a very special type of labour contract.

461. Besides that, the WSA regulates also the ' contract in training practices to obtain professional practice' ('contrato formativo para la obtención de la práctica profesional'); the executive rules are in the Article 11.3 WSA and in Royal Decree 488/1998, of 27 March. The rules of both contracts must be studied.

462. A contract for work-linked training may be held with people who lack the professional qualification recognized by the degrees or certificates required to conclude a training contract to obtain professional practice; also linked to vocational or university training studies with people who have another qualification as long as they have not had another previous training contract in training at the same training level and in the same productive sector. However, if the purpose of the contract is some of the training specialities recognized by the Spanish National Employment System, it can only be concluded with people up to 30 years of age.

463. The duration of the labour contract will be that provided for in the corresponding training plan or program, with a minimum of three months and a maximum of two years, and may be developed under a single contract on a non-continuous basis, over various coinciding annual periods with the studies, if provided for in the training plan or program. In the event that the labour contract had been concluded for a duration less than the established legal maximum and the title, certificate, accreditation or diploma associated with the training contract had not been obtained, it may be extended by agreement of the parties, until said title, certificate, accreditation or diploma is obtained without ever exceeding the maximum duration of two years.

464. Other rules to consider in relation to this type of labour contract are the following:

– The activity carried out by the employee in the company must be directly related to the training activities that justify the labour contract, coordinating and integrating into a common training program, prepared within the framework of the cooperation agreements and agreements signed by the labour authorities or educational vocational training or Universities with collaborating companies and entities.

- Both the theoretical training provided by the training centre or entity or the company itself, when established, and the corresponding practical training provided by the company and the centre are a substantial part of this labour contract.
- The effective working time, which must be compatible with the time dedicated to training activities at the training centre, may not exceed 65%, during the first year, or 85%, during the second, the maximum working day provided for in the collective agreement applicable to the company, or, failing that, the maximum legal working day.
- The people hired may not work complementary hours or overtime, except in some cases expressly provided for by law. They will also not be able to do night work, shift work, or be subjected to a trial period.
- Contracts for worklinked training cannot be concluded when the activity or job corresponding to the labour contract has been previously carried out by the employee in the same company under any modality for a period of more than six months.
- The wage will be that established for these labour contracts in the applicable collective agreement. In the absence of conventional provision, the wage may not be less than 60% in the first year or 75% in the second, with respect to that established in the agreement for the professional group and remuneration level corresponding to the functions performed, in proportion to effective working time. In no case may the wage be less than the minimum interprofessional salary in proportion to the actual working time.
- The hired person will have a tutor designated by the training centre or entity and another designated by the company.

465. A contract in training practices to obtain professional practice is provided for persons with a university or technical degree, in order to perfect their knowledge. Considering the situation of the labour market, this has been qualified as an effective way to insert young workers into employment. In any case, the workplace must permit the professional practice appropriate to the level of studies or training of the employee.

The contract must be put in writing. It is a temporary contract, with a minimum of six months and a maximum of one year. It can only be concluded up to three years after a professional degree has been obtained or; up to five years when the employee is handicapped.

466. This labour contract cannot be signed with someone who has already obtained professional experience or carried out training activity in the same activity within the company for a period of more than three months, without the training or internship periods that are part of the curriculum being counted for these purposes required to obtain the degree or certificate that enables this contract.

467. Wages will be that established in the collective agreement applicable in the company for these contracts or, failing that, that of the professional group and remuneration level corresponding to the functions performed. In no case may the wage be less than the minimum remuneration established for the contract for work-linked training, nor the minimum wage in proportion to the actual working time. The WSA establishes two other rights of the employee related to his training:

- If the employee studies for a university or professional degree, he has the right to absences from his work to sit examinations, and a right to choose his shift when there are several in the shop. Although there is debate about whether this absence should be paid – the law does not make it explicit –, Spanish courts have generally recognized that permission for an employee to take an exam for a university degree must be considered paid.
- If the employee follows courses of professional training, he has a right to an accommodation of his working day or to a licence, which means a suspension of his contract, with a supplementary right to reinstatement at his work place.

468. In general terms, the following can be referred to in both contractual modalities:

- Social Security protects these contracts in the same way as it does other contractual modalities, so today they do not have inferior protection, something that did happen in the past. Likewise, situations of temporary disability, birth, adoption, custody for adoption purposes, foster care, risk during pregnancy, risk during breastfeeding, and gender violence, interrupt the calculation of the duration of the labour contract.
- The age limits and maximum duration of training contracts will not apply when the employee is a person with a disability or belongs to groups in a situation of social exclusion. In this sense, these training contracts operate as a kind of contractual modality for the labour insertion of certain groups.
- If at the end of the training contract, the person continues in the company, it will not be possible to establish a new trial period, and the duration of the training contract will count for seniority purposes.
- When appreciated that the training contract was concluded in fraud of the law, or the company fails to comply with its training obligations with respect to them, said contracts entered into will be considered indefinite contracts of an ordinary nature, with the corresponding legal effects of this contractual modality

§4. Handicapped Persons

469. Most of the rules about handicapped persons, especially in the case of severe incapacity, are regulated within the Social Security Act as part of its benefits. Special employment centres of the Ministry of Labour and Social Economy or, with its financial assistance, are established by public or private institutions.

470. An Act of 29 November 2013 regulates the 'rights of persons with disabilities and their social inclusion' (Royal Legislative Decree 1/2013); among other rules, the Act includes an explicit prohibition of discrimination in employment and labour conditions by reason of being a handicapped person; promotion of special centres for those who cannot work in normal conditions; and promotion of their employment in public and private enterprises.

471. Other special rules protect these workers, namely on employment (reserves and preferences of work places) and on safe conditions of work.

472. As we have seen (Chapter 1, §1), the contract of handicapped persons who are employed in special centres is recognized as one of the so-called special labour relationships. The Act of 29 November 2013 establishes special provisions for this.

473. In 2023, the Employment Act recovered the equality of those who have a recognized permanent disability pension in a total, absolute or major degree of disability, to people who have a degree of disability equal to or greater than 33%, which will allow them to access the benefits and labour regime provided for this last group.

§5. Migrant Workers

474. As was said at the beginning, emigration is an important topic within Spanish labour law and within Spanish social relationships generally. In the past, most emigration occurred towards Latin American countries and there are still a high number of people holding Spanish passports and nationality in those countries. Colombia is the most important country of reception, Argentina, Venezuela and Brazil also have high figures. Beginning in the mid-1950s, and up to the mid-1970s, there was a significant current of emigration to western European countries (towards France, the movement is much older; it actually began at the turn of the nineteenth century). More than a million Spanish people lived and worked in different countries of Europe, with France leading followed by the Federal Republic of Germany and Switzerland.

Changes in the Spanish economic situation have caused a significant reduction in those numbers, with many workers who lived and worked abroad returning to Spain. Recently this has been accompanied by the important and significant migration of foreign people to Spain, especially from the Maghreb and Eastern Europe. The Spanish Emigration Act now in force (40/2006, 14 December, on the Statute of Spanish citizens abroad) establishes the legal framework for Spanish citizens living outside Spain, and its purpose is the legal guarantee of the exercise of their constitutional rights and duties, on equal terms with the Spanish residents in the national territory. In addition, it aims to strengthen the links of these citizens with Spain, and improve the conditions of life of the Spanish residents abroad, in those areas where the existing protection in the country of residence may need to be completed. The law is applicable to citizens who hold Spanish citizenship and reside outside the national territory; to those who move temporarily – excluding those who do so in the exercise of the right to free movement of employees recognized by the European Union; and to the families of these citizens – including unmarried partners.

475. The Emigration Act is mostly concerned with the protection of the emigrant before leaving the country, during his travel, and in his living in the foreign country. Actually, protection in the foreign country is mostly guaranteed under the bilateral treaties which Spain has signed with most western European and South American countries. The basic clause of these agreements is that the Spanish worker in the country of immigration (and the worker of the country of emigration in Spain) will have the same labour rights as the national of the country to which he emigrates. Additional and also bilateral social security treaties cover this very important part of the protection.

476. As far as the European Union countries are concerned, we must remember the application of the free movement of workers' rule.

477. Miscellaneous executive decrees and orders have been promulgated to aid the returning emigrant in matters such as public housing occupancy and ownership, education for himself and his dependants, convertible saving accounts, etc.

§6. Protection Against Discrimination in Employment

478. The quite specific reference in the title of this paragraph, 'in employment', leaves outside the scope of our consideration here protection in general against discrimination, contained mainly in the two United Nations Basic Human Rights Treaties, and specifically against racial discrimination in the United Nations Declaration of 20 November 1963, and in the Convention on the Elimination of Every Form of Radical Discrimination of 21 December 1965.

479. Nevertheless, the specific provisions against discrimination 'in employment' shall be understood as being a part of the general protection against discrimination in civil, political, social, economic, and cultural fields; and the possible lack of a certain provision barring a certain type of discrimination in employment must be consequently understood as filled by the application of the above-named conventions, all of them ratified by Spain. We can pass, thus, two specific norms.

I. Protection Against Discrimination for Trade Union Membership and Activities

480. The TUA declares null and void any act of discrimination related to employment, against trade union freedom. That includes especially the will to include in the labour contract the duty not to join a union or to leave it; and any prejudice because of union membership or participation in union activities (*see* Part II, Chapter 1).

481. Special reference should be made to discriminatory dismissal because of union membership. There is no manifest prohibition in the WSA; it is clear however that it is covered by the general prohibition that declares 'null and void' employers' unilateral decisions that should contain unfavourable discriminations because of union membership or participation in union activities.

II. Protection Against Discrimination by Reason of Sex

482. As stated above in Chapter 1, §2(V), there are no limitations due to sex or marital status against entry into a labour contract. Earlier in this chapter we referred to the special protection of female workers. There are two major legal provisions.

i. As for dismissal for reason of sex, the same general rule of the WSA seen above is applied: the employer's unilateral decision which contains discrimination by reason of sex is null and void.
ii. Article 28 WSA says that the employer 'is obliged to pay for the provision of work of equal value the same remuneration, paid directly or indirectly, and whatever the nature of the remuneration, whether salary or extra-salary, without any discrimination on the basis of sex in any case. of the elements or conditions of that'. Of course, the decrees about inter-professional minimum wages, do not make any difference between a male and a female in establishing minimum general, wages. The collective bargaining agreement attempting to establish different scales of wages will be void and the scale applied will be the higher one for both sexes.

483. In any case, in recent years the legislator has reinforced the fight against discrimination based on sex, especially in salary matters, providing specific legal criteria for such purposes, as is the case of the following legal provision contained in Article 28 WSA: 'A job will have equal value to another when the nature of the functions or tasks actually entrusted, the educational, professional or training conditions required for its exercise, the factors strictly related to its performance and the working conditions in which said activities are carried out are actually equivalent.'

484. An Act of 22 March 2007 (Organic Act 3/2007) provides measures 'for the effective equality of women and men', not only in labour relations. Among other rules, it obliges enterprises with fifty or more employees to negotiate with employees' representatives an 'equality plan' including specific objectives and measures to eliminate sex discrimination. A similar legal obligation has been established in the case of employees belonging to the LGBTQ + collective, so from now on companies with fifty or more employees are obliged to develop a specific plan (equality plan) that promotes equality, and facilitates the protection of this group.

III. Protection Against Other Types of Discrimination

485. The much-quoted rule of the WSA against discrimination declares null and void the employers' unilateral decisions mentioned above and also those related to situations of direct or indirect unfavourable discrimination due to age or disability or to situations of direct or indirect discrimination due to sex, origin, including race or ethnicity, marital status, social condition, religion or convictions, political ideas, sexual orientation and identity, gender expression, sexual characteristics, membership or not to unions and their agreements, kinship ties with people belonging to or related to the company and language within of the Spanish State. There is no doubt that the rule must and also will be applied to dismissal and to any type of discrimination other than dismissal.

Chapter 8. Duty of Secrecy and Covenants of Non-competition

§1. Duty of Secrecy

486. The Labour Contract Act of 1944, today derogated, stated the employee's duty to maintain the secrets which refer to the works and business of his employer; this duty did not end with the termination of the contract but existed even after this. The WSA does not contain a similar rule but we can maintain that the duty exists today implicit in the employee's duties derived from the labour contract itself.

487. Certainly the duty is an absolute duty, in the sense that it has no temporal limitation at all; provided the 'secrecy' is taken in the strict sense of the word, meaning something which cannot possibly be known without having entered into the 'guarded zone' or someone's intimate confidence.

488. But whether the violation of the secret has been committed during the life of the labour contract or after its termination, does have important effects not in labour but in criminal law. 'Anyone who reveals other people's secrets, of which they have knowledge due to their job or their labour relationships,' is a crime described in the Penal Code (Article 199.1), which is punishable by a prison sentence of one to three years, and a fine; among other persons, the employer is protected against violation of the secrets of the enterprise by employees in accordance with the best authorities; (a) during the life of the labour contract there is a general protection, while (b) after the contract is terminated the crime only exists if it is committed through the disclosure of classified documents which the employee has obtained, or surreptitiously taken, by reason of or by taking advantage of, his employment.

489. Coming back to labour law, the duty to keep the secrets exists whether or not, through the revelation, the employee obtains for himself a profit or the profit if any accrues to a third party. The same rule applies incidentally to the duty not to compete studied below.

490. If there is a breach of his duty by the employee he can be dismissed because such conduct will be deemed to be a cause of disloyalty or breach of the bona fides which justifies the dismissal.

491. Besides the employer has a right to be indemnified for any damages due to the breach of secrecy, even if it is committed as was said, after termination of the labour contract.

492. In any case, different EU initiatives in recent years have determined that the Spanish legislator promotes laws that in some cases enhance this duty of secrecy, and in others qualify it. Thus, first, and in the development of Directive (EU) 2016/943, Spanish legislation (Act 1/2019 of 20 February) prohibits any person from obtaining, using, or disclosing a business secret without the consent of its owner. In fact, it considers an infringement, or unfair practice, any conduct that pursues the misappropriation of business secrets, such as theft, unauthorized copying, economic espionage, or non-compliance with confidentiality requirements, and which will be prosecuted in the legal field. For Spanish law, business secrets include 'any information that is secret, has business value and has been subject to reasonable measures by its owner to keep it secret'.

493. Second, and in this case in the development of Directive (EU) 2019/1937, Spanish law regulates the protection of those known as 'whistleblowers', as people who, in a labour or professional context, detect criminal infractions, or serious administrative offences or very serious, establishing for this purpose the corresponding information channels, with the corresponding guarantees of confidentiality regarding the origin of the information, so that said people can report the aforementioned infractions, either to the organizations that commit the infraction, to act diligently to correct the situation, or to the government authorities when deemed appropriate.

§2. Covenants of Non-competition

494. The situation during and after the termination of the contract should be distinguished.

495. During the contract the general formulation of the WSA is as follows: 'The services of the employee shall not be provided to several employers if it could be regarded as disloyal competition.'

As disloyal competition we mean work in activities of the same nature, or in the same line of business, as that being done in carrying out the labour contract because of a violation of the bona fides principle.

Probably, although this thesis cannot be established as completely settled, the competition, in order to be forbidden, needs to involve an element of actual or potential damage to the employer, because without this element the prohibition will mean an invasion of the principle of freedom of work and even of basic human freedom. And if the actual or potential damage exists there is a legal interest which can be protected and that in fact is protected by the law. What the employee is not allowed to do is to 'put himself in a situation in which he is solicited by two contradictory interests', as stated in a Supreme Court decision. Of course, this duty of the employee is an implied duty; its exigency can be condoned by the employer giving his explicit or tacit consent to the 'competitive work'.

A violation of the duty not to compete is a cause for justified dismissal of the employee. But the simple fact of having 'contacts or conversation', but no more than that, with another employer who is a competitor, is not by itself prohibited competition.

496. After the contract, as we have seen above, the use by the former employee of the experience acquired in his employment, just like the normal experience of anyone who works in a profession or trade, cannot be forbidden. Apart from this, the duty of non-competition cannot be longer than two years, if the employee is a 'technician' meaning by that a highly qualified, usually non-manual worker, and no longer than six months for other personnel.

497. The prolongation of the duty during the said periods has to be agreed upon with the former employee, and the employer shall agree to pay 'an indemnity' during the said period; if the parties do not agree on its amount the Labour Court fixes it.

498. The WSA governs the so-called Full dedication agreement, which eliminates the right of the employee to work for other employers; the employee has a right in this case to economic compensation and can recuperate his freedom to work for others if he communicates it to the employer in a thirty-day period.

Chapter 9. Inventions by Employees

499. The legal rules regarding an employee's invention are not given by labour law but by the general Patent Act 24/2015, of 24 July.

Three types of inventions within the labour relationship may be considered.

500. The first type is inventions made by employees whose labour contract calls explicitly or implicitly to study and try to obtain them; they are the so-called service inventions. The invention itself, so to speak, is the object of the labour contract.

The invention belongs to the employer, the employee has no right to a supplementary remuneration if there is no specific agreement. But if the invention itself has a value exceeding the object of the labour contract, economic compensation is due.

501. The second type includes inventions made by employees not employed to invent, that are beyond the object, explicit or implicit, of his labour contract. These free inventions belong to the employee. Furthermore, an agreement made prior to the invention to renounce this type of property is null and void.

502. The last type are inventions principally due to knowledge, skills or experience of the employee in the enterprise, or making use of the processes, installations or methods of the enterprise (factory inventions). The employer has a right to appropriate them or to use them and the employee has a right to reasonable economic compensation which shall be fixed according to the importance of the invention, of the knowledge or methods provided by the employer and the value of the employee's contribution.

503. The Patent Act establishes a duty upon two parties to collaborate and contribute to making effective the rights corresponding to them.

Disputes on the matter are decided by the civil, not labour, courts.

504. What has just been said applies to what generally can be called technical or industrial inventions. If the invention is of literary, artistic or scientific nature – like a book or a musical composition – the Intellectual Property Act, Royal Legislative Decree 1/1996, of 12 April, applies.

Within the labour relationship, the work belongs to the employee, the contract can transfer the exploitation rights to the employer with an economic compensation to the employee.

Chapter 10. Settlement of Disputes

§1. Introduction

505. As Part I considers only the individual employment relationship, this chapter deals only with the settlement of individual labour disputes. Collective industrial disputes will be studied in Part II, Chapter 5. This is not the occasion to delve into the highly technical and even dogmatic problem of what is an individual dispute as opposed to a collective one, nor to delve into the related distinction between a legal or juridical dispute as opposed to an economic one. It is sufficient to say that, generally speaking, an individual dispute is one which arises between a single employee and his employer (in matters relating to the labour relationship). If in order to consider a dispute as collective you add to the collective fact the need that the dispute shall affect the collectivity as a whole, infringing upon the rights or interests of the group as such, then there is the need to allow for a tertium genus of so-called plural disputes, in which several individual workers are affected at the same time but neither as a whole nor as standard-bearers, so to speak, for the interest of the group. Plural disputes are deemed to be individual disputes.

506. Individual disputes are usually and mainly legal disputes, in the sense that, although economic individual disputes between employer and employee are conceivable, the dispute lacks the 'social pressure' or 'social impact' which is behind the law and regulations existing to deal with collective economic disputes.

507. The main characteristic of the Spanish system for the settlement of individual disputes is a highly developed and popular system of Labour Courts. But before entering into the study of the organization and proceedings before the Labour Courts which are the gist of this chapter, reference should be made to other possible types of grievance procedure.

§2. Arbitration, Mediation, Conciliation

508. Arbitration for individual labour complaints is almost unknown in Spain. For a long time, there were serious doubts as to whether it was even legally possible at all. The Arbitration Act, on the one hand, excluded labour questions from its field; on the other, the courts repeatedly and strongly maintained that it is a basic individual right pertaining to every employee to appear before the Labour Court with his complaint and that this right cannot be either denied or unreasonably delayed.

509. More recently, this doctrine has been abandoned and arbitration in individual disputes is accepted, but its application remains limited. This means of settling labour complaints has actually little traditional application in labour relations, which partially explains its lack of use.

510. The most important institution in this field is the 'mandatory previous conciliation', as a necessary previous proceeding to every claim before Labour Courts; certain claims are excluded from this rule; disputes on social security, matters on elections of representatives of the employees in the enterprise, disputes in which the state and another public person act as parties.

511. The conciliation proceedings follow before the labour administration. It is very simplified with the following steps; written initiation of proceedings, appearance of the parties before the conciliator (a public official), and attempt at agreement. The result of the proceedings, positive or negative, must be put in writing, including in the case of a positive outcome the agreement reached.

512. Of course, if the conciliation attempt has a positive end, the parties have avoided proceedings before the Labour Court. The law says that the agreement has 'an executive effect'. But if agreement has not been possible, the parties can proceed before the court.

513. This type of conciliation renders good service in discharging, through conciliation, part of the enormous work load of the Labour Courts.

514. In collective bargaining agreements it is mandatory to include a clause setting up a mixed employer – employee committee 'to deal with all matters it may be called upon'. Although mainly thought of in the context of collective disputes, the general clause refers also to disputes and appears as a form of conciliation or mediation.

515. There is conciliation before the Labour Court itself, but this is part of the Labour Court proceedings and will be studied below.

§3. The Labour Courts

516. The Labour Court system will be studied under the following headings:

- organization of the Labour Courts;
- jurisdiction of the Labour Courts;
- the parties before the Labour Courts;
- general and special proceedings before the Labour Courts;
- appeals against Labour Court decisions.

517. The treatment of all these topics will be made in a very schematic way. Because the system of Labour Courts is old and important there are many thousands of decisions dealing directly or indirectly with procedural labour problems; out of them a highly specialized branch of law, midway between labour and (civil) procedural law, has emerged, with courses, books, and doctoral dissertations under the general heading procedural labour law.

518. The last part of the chapter will deal with the statute of limitations applicable to labour actions.

I. Organization of the Labour Courts

519. The Labour Court system is formed by the Juzgado de lo Social (Labour Court), Sala de lo Social de los Tribunales Superiores de Justicia (Social Chamber of the Autonomous Regions Courts of Justice), Sala de lo Social de la Audiencia Nacional (Social Chamber of the National Court of Justice) and Sala de lo Social del Tribunal Supremo (Social Chamber of the Supreme Court).

520. The Labour Court is composed of a labour judge (Juez de lo Social) and auxiliary personnel (among them the Lawyer of the Administration of Justice – formerly known as Secretary of the Labour Court – a highly specialized lawyer). There exists at least one Labour Court in every one of the fifty provinces of Spain, located in the capital of the province. Many provinces have more than one. Different cities which are not provincial capitals, but which are important industrial centres, have Labour Courts.

The labour judge is from the legal profession, pertaining to a unitary body with the rest of the civil, criminal and administrative judges.

521. The Social Chamber of the Autonomous Regions Court of Justice is formed by a President and several judges. Some of the courts have two or three Social Chambers.

522. The Social Chamber of the Audiencia Nacional is formed by a President and two judges.

523. The Social Chamber of the Supreme Court is formed by a President and twelve judges. Three and no more than three members must concur for a decision to be reached. In certain cases, the President or a majority of judges can decide that five members or even all of them must concur.

524. Needless to say, provincial judges, and justices, cannot be removed nor transferred for any reason (except by impeachment because of crime, whose adjudication is reserved to the Supreme Court).

II. Jurisdiction of the Labour Courts

525. Primary jurisdiction on labour cases belongs to the labour judges; higher courts within the labour jurisdictional structure are only involved in appeals against decisions of the labour judges. That being the case, the following suggests itself as an order to study the topic of jurisdiction.

A. Jurisdiction of the Provincial Labour Judges

526. Labour judges have primary jurisdiction in individual conflicts emerging from labour and social security relationships. Leaving aside social security cases (although it must be said that they take up a very important part of the time and effort of the labour judges), the jurisdiction over labour cases extends, with minor exceptions, to every dispute between employer and employee that has as its source, directly or indirectly, the labour relationship; wages and every type of remunerations, hours of work, vacations and rest periods, labour conditions generally, dismissals and other forms of termination of the labour contract, damages deriving from them, etc., and related matters that can be submitted to the Labour Court for a decision, by either party. These are cases of 'individual' – or plural, in the sense already mentioned – disputes as opposed to 'collective' ones. Collective disputes also belong to the jurisdiction of the labour judge, provided they are legal or juridical disputes, i.e., the matter of the dispute is the application or the interpretation of a pre-existing norm, be it strictly legal, that is emanating from the State, or contained in a collective bargaining agreement.

527. Coming back to a topic already discussed, it should be said that the distinction between individual and collective disputes is not as clear as the terminology may suggest; actually, not infrequently a series of individual complaints amount to a collective dispute although they tend to be treated in law as individual ones. So much so that there has appeared between individual and collective the so-called plural disputes as a species of the individual disputes. Only when it is absolutely clear that a collective interest, pertaining to a group of employees as such, is prima facie affected, will the labour judge insist on following the special proceedings established for collective disputes (declaring his lack of jurisdiction if the dispute, besides being collective, is an economic one).

528. However, it should be noted that it is possible for the same matter to be heard by two different jurisdictions, logically from different perspectives. An example of this is litigation regarding strikes, where the contentious-administrative jurisdiction hears the objections that may arise in relation to the administrative resolution that establishes the minimum services that must be respected in a strike called in an activity that is considered an essential service since the social jurisdiction will assess the possible consequences of certain decisions of the employer in relation to its employees during the strike.

529. Among the various labour judges the jurisdiction is given according to mainly territorial criteria. In the usual cases, the plaintiff can complain before the labour judge of the province in which the place of work is located or in which the employer has his legal residence. Among the labour judges within the same province, the cases are distributed simply by numerical order assigned to the cases as they enter the docks.

530. Perhaps it will be convenient to say that the Juzgado de lo Social, the labour judges, are very popular in Spain in the sense that use is made of them in a very high number of cases. In 2023, labour judges have annually disposed of an average of more than 340,837 cases (including, one must remember, social security cases) and the number is most likely to increase in the near future.

B. *Jurisdiction of Higher Tribunals*

531. There are decisions of the Labour Courts for which there is no appeal. Generally speaking, there is no appeal against a Labour Court decision when the amount involved in the case is less than EUR 3,000 unless a point of gross infringement of procedural law is raised or if one of the parties says, and duly proves, that the amount under discussion will affect a great number of employees (or a great number of insured persons). Apart from the amount of the case, there is no appeal in disputes on the effective date of annual vacation, election of employees' representatives in the enterprise, professional classification of the employee and minor sanctions applied by the employer to the employee.

532. Jurisdiction of higher tribunals is partially primary and partially in the form of an appeal against the decisions of other courts. A distinction should be made between them.

533. The Social Chamber of the Regional Court of Justice has primary jurisdiction in conflicts which in principle belong to the Labour Court when they exceed the provincial territory and do not transcend the regional territory. It also has appellate jurisdiction over decisions of the Labour Courts when the amount of the case is more than EUR 3,000. Basically, in this second case, the appeal is on points of law, substantive or procedural. There is also a certain re-examination on points of facts if the appellant bases his appeal on errors deriving from, precisely, the documents or professional expertise incorporated in the proceedings before the Labour Judge.

534. The Social Chamber of the Audiencia Nacional had primary jurisdiction in conflicts which in principle belong to the Regional Court of Justice when they transcend the territory of the Region. These conflicts are mostly collective ones, in the sense we have seen above.

535. The Social Chamber of the Supreme Court only has appellate jurisdiction over appeals against the decisions of the Social Chambers of the Regional Court of Justice or of the Social Chamber of the Audiencia Nacional.

536. Both the Social Chamber of the Regional Court of Justice and the Social Chamber of the Supreme will decide on appeal either giving their own opinions in the case or remanding it to the Court below for further consideration.

537. Again, an enormous amount of work has to be shouldered by these High Labour Courts; the Social Chambers of the Regional Courts decide over 48,000 cases in 2023; the Fourth Chamber of the Supreme Court decides over 1,323 cases in that same year.

538. Although the topic of court decisions as a source of Labour Law has already been studied (*see* Introduction, Chapter 5, §9), we shall mention here their historical and present importance in the configuration of labour law. Other things apart, the Labour Courts in reasoning over their own jurisdiction had many times, for instance, to decide if what was before them was a labour contract or a work-connected accident, and so delve deeply and finely into its elements and nature. And now, in the middle of rapidly changing enactments, court decisions give some basic stable ground to the jurist and provide for the continuity of labour law elaboration.

C. The Parties Before the Labour Courts

539. Employees can appear before the Labour Court if they are 18 years of age or older; if they are under 18 they must be represented by their legal representatives or guardians. Both parties may appear by themselves or be represented by any person of 18 years of age or more in full possession of his legal capacity. This means that no solicitor, barrister, or attorney at law is necessary, although in most cases the parties do use the legal service of an attorney who, in the case of employees, is perhaps provided by their unions. For appeals before higher tribunals, the appointment of an attorney is necessary.

D. General and Special Proceedings Before the Labour Courts

540. Procedural labour law provides for 'general proceedings' for most usual cases and 'special proceedings' for some types of cases; although the speciality generally refers to very minor points (except perhaps in social security cases). There is no charge for the proceedings which in part explains why so much use is made of them. The general proceeding follows six main steps:

1. The complaint must be submitted in writing, stating the names and addresses of the parties, the facts of the case and the decision which is asked from the Court.
2. The Labour Court makes an initial, simple analysis of the complaint and if it is deemed to be within its jurisdiction it orders the appearance of both parties before it for a hearing at a certain place, date and hour (if the matter is clearly not within the jurisdiction of the Labour Court, it must be so decided without further delay). If the Labour Court observes defects in the complaint the party is directed to correct them within four days.
3. The hearing begins with the labour judge sitting as a conciliator and mediator who tries to obtain – and very frequently does obtain – an agreement between the parties, although he cannot accept, much less propose, an agreement which is prejudicial to one of the parties.
4. If conciliation is not reached, the hearing proper then begins. This is in four stages:
   - The plaintiff ratifies his complaint; he can reduce it, and can even modify it, provided it is not a 'substantial' modification.

- The defendant opposes the complaint using at this moment every type of defence, either procedural or substantive, as to the facts or the law.
- The elements of proof are introduced at this moment; documents are presented, parties and witnesses are examined and cross-examined, and experts are also examined and cross-examined (although affidavits of an expert's written report can be introduced). Any objection concerning proofs is decided outright by the labour judge who is empowered to examine the parties and the witnesses. If an objection is not admitted, a protest may be entered into the record for future use in an appeal.
- After the examination period has ended the plaintiffs and the defendant make their final statements.

5. The labour judge delivers his decision in writing within five days following the hearing. He may give his decision orally just after the end of the hearing, except in some cases because of the more complex contents of the decision: disciplinary dismissals, termination of the labour contract due to the will of the employee, dismissals due to objective causes, collective disputes and others.
6. Exceptionally the judge may deem it necessary to order new and additional proof, either on his own insistence or following the recommendation of the parties. In such a case, time is allowed for that to be completed.

541. As we have said, the so-called special proceedings mostly follow the general one. Special proceedings are, mainly, those of dismissals, employer's sanctions and social security cases. One of the most important and peculiar special proceedings is where the complaint emanates not from the party himself but from some labour authority, usually, the labour inspector, who during his inspection has discovered breaches of labour law which give the employee a legal right to complain. The labour inspector prepares and sends the complaint to the labour judge, but further activities of the Court are entertained with the affected parties. A special proceeding is also provided for collective disputes; it will be dealt with in Part II, Chapter 6.

E. Appeals to Higher Tribunals

542. It is sufficient to say that appeals are in writing; that the appellant must be heard; that the appeals are mostly on point of law, in the main substantial points but occasionally procedural; that mistakes of fact concerning the appreciation of expertise and documents may also be made the object of the appeal, and very frequently are, but that no new proof can be introduced at this stage; and that the superior court can either confirm or rescind the decision of the Labour Court. In the latter case, it either reaches its own decision or remands the case to the labour judge for him to decide anew. Peremptory judicial decisions of the Labour Court negating its jurisdiction can also be appealed, the higher court deciding, then, merely the jurisdictional problem and remanding the case to the lower court for determination if its original decision is rescinded.

543. A very peculiar appeal is the so-called appeal for the unification of judicial doctrine (recurso de casación para la unificación de doctrina), against decisions of the Social Chambers of the Regional Court of Justice before the Social Chamber of the Supreme Court. Its purpose is to unify the interpretation of labour law, eliminating contradictions between decisions of the Regional Courts of Justice or between these decisions and the decisions of the Supreme Court. This appeal is only on points of law, substantive or procedural.

544. Exceptionally, and only when it is considered an infringement of fundamental rights or public freedoms, it will be possible to file an appeal for protection before the Constitutional Court against a final judicial decision. However, to present said appeal it is necessary that all possible remedies in the ordinary social jurisdiction have been exhausted, including, where appropriate, the aforementioned 'recurso de casación para la unificación de doctrina' heard by the Supreme Court.

§4. Statute of Limitations

545. This is as good a place as any other, we think, to deal with the important subject of the statute of limitations; perhaps it is actually the best place because matters pertaining to it tend to appear precisely when a complaint is presented to the Labour Court.

546. The general rule is that a one-year statute of limitations period applies to every labour complaint; with the very important provision that the term starts from the day on which the labour contract is terminated and not before; unless the complaint is about wages and remuneration in which case the one year term starts from the date on which the wages were due and not paid, or not paid in full.

547. The rule about the starting date on which the complaint could be presented also applies to complaints concerning rights not realizable after the termination of the labour contract; which refers to the annual vacation period.

548. In cases of dismissals the statute of limitations is very short and drastic: twenty days from the date of the dismissal. Of course, the reason for such a short term is that the law wants to have any controversy about dismissal decided as clearly and as quickly as possible. An additional rule to that end is that no other complaint can be added to a complaint concerning dismissal, to prevent an employee from aggregating into a single complaint every dispute he has with his employer.

549. In writing about the disciplinary power of the employer (*see* above, Chapter 2) reference was made to the statute of limitations as applied to this power. Article 60 of the WSA rules this matter, which can be summarized in two points.

i. If the employer knows about the act of the employee, he must exercise his powers to discipline within ten, twenty or sixty days from the date of his knowledge. These periods of time are applied, respectively, to minor, serious, or very serious faults (classifications of faults in the three groups usually appear in the applicable collective agreement). Only a very serious fault can give reason for dismissal and, thus, the employer must dismiss within the sixty days following the date on which the breach which he is going to use in support of his decision came to his knowledge.

ii. But 'in any case', i.e., whether the employer knows it or not, a general statute of limitations of six months from its commission applies to any act of the employee, as a last temporal limit to the employer's power to discipline.

Part II. Collective Labour Relations

Introduction

550. At the beginning of this exposition, we made some reference to what we called 'temporal background', explaining in a general way the changes which for thirty years have affected, in particular, the collective side of labour and industrial relationships in Spain. Landmarks of this change have been the long overdue ratification by Spain not only of the so-called Basic United Nations Treaties on Human Rights but, more precisely, also ILO Conventions No. 87 on Trade Union Freedom and Protection of the Right to Unionize, and No. 98 on the Rights to Unionize and to Collective Bargaining. More important was the approval of the Constitution in December 1978, which recognizes and guarantees basic rights in this matter (right to unionize, right to strike, right to collective bargaining).

551. Even before the ratification of the conventions, one of the very last important acts approved by the old Cortes was Act 19/1977 of 1 April about the right to unionize, preceding the ratification and actually allowing for it and, at the same time, preceding the Constitution itself, which today contains the basic rules on this matter.

552. The coming into force of the Constitution implied the definitive recovery of trade union freedom, meaning a partial return to the pre-1939 situation: freedom to create trade unions, and freedom to join a trade union. As a result, trade union freedom led to a plurality of organizations. Some of them are 'historical' ones, with a long and important evolution up until 1939, reappearing in 1977 after a clandestine and illegal period in which they survived, diminished and in very difficult conditions. Others were not only new, created after 1939, but also illegal; or after 1977, when the above-mentioned Act about the right to unionize was approved.

553. After 1958 (between 1939 and this date there was no legal means to do this) there began the important development of collective bargaining, within the official trade union structure. Collective agreements, since then, have played an increasing part in the regulation of labour conditions. Until 1977, however, the possibility was severely limited: on the one hand, the law set important limitations on the content of the agreements; on the other hand, a strong control of the collective bargaining process was carried out by administrative and public trade unions. As we have said, the Constitution contains the guarantee of trade union activity and collective bargaining, which of course reinforces its role in the regulation of labour conditions and collective labour relations. Today, collective bargaining and collective agreements are regulated in the ES.

554. During the life of the old trade union structure – i.e., until 1977 – there was a system of institutionalized relations between employees and employer in the enterprise, through representatives elected by the former. Regulations approved after the Constitution has established a very similar system, at least regarding the functions of the representative institutions. An essential difference, however, must be indicated: these institutions do not belong to the trade union structure, as the preceding ones did. The general situation of trade union freedom and plurality is also an important change in this matter.

555. Industrial conflict was of course frequent in a relatively highly industrialized country like Spain, and legislation, beginning with strikes and other forms of industrial conflict, had to admit the fact, each time in more ample and realistic terms. The years 1962, 1970, 1975 and 1977 saw the appearance of complete regulations of collective conflicts, each one trying to be more progressive than its predecessor. The 1977 legislation begins with the formal declaration that there is a right to strike – any clause to the contrary in the labour contract being null and void (which can be renounced only through a collective bargaining agreement and only while it is in force).

556. The Constitution recognizes the right to strike as one of the essential rights of employees. No other regulation of collective conflicts has appeared since then; it was doubtful if the regulation of 1977 – prior to the Constitution, we must remember – was then in force. The Constitutional Court has answered this important question; its decision has determined which part of this regulation has been abolished by the Constitution and which part is still in force. This topic will be examined below.

Chapter 1. Trade Union Freedom, Trade Unions and Employers' Associations

§1. Introduction

557. Article 28 of the Constitution says:

> Every one has the right to unionize freely. Trade union freedom includes the right to form trade unions and the right to belong to the one of their own choosing; the right of the trade unions to form confederations and international unions and to join them. Nobody is obliged to join a trade union.

Article 7 says:

> Trade unions and employees' associations contribute to the defence and promotion of their own economic and social interests. Their foundation and their activity are free, with respect to the Constitution and to the law.

These rules mean that trade union freedom includes collective and individual freedoms (i.e., to form trade unions and join them), both positive and negative freedoms (i.e., to join and not to join a union). Perhaps, the insistence of the Constitution on negative freedom is due to previous, pre-constitutional experience of mandatory unionization in official trade unions; it also prevents, as we will see below, the enforcement of union membership in a contract.

558. ILO Conventions nos 87 and 98 were both ratified by Spain in 1977 and they have become the law of the land. United Nations Conventions on Civil and Political Rights and on Economic, Social and Cultural Rights have also been ratified. Both Conventions, it is well known, provide for the right to 'every person to freely associate with others including the right to form unions and belong to them for the protection of their interests' (Article 22, Convention on Civil and Political Rights) and for the right of every person to 'establish unions and belong to one of their own choosing' and 'the right to the unions themselves to form federations, to belong to international federations and to generally function without any obstacle or limitation except those legally established and compatible with the principles of democratic society' (Article 8, Economic, Social and Cultural Rights Convention). These texts have clearly inspired Articles 7 and 28 of the Spanish Constitution.

§2. Trade Union Regulation

559. Apart from the constitutional rules mentioned above, the basic legal text about trade unions is 11/1985, of 2 August, TUA. Reproducing the declaration of the Constitution, Article 1 of the TUA says that 'every employee has the right to unionize freely for the promotion and defence of his economic and social interests'.

The Act adds that trade union freedom includes the right to form trade unions, the right to join them, the right to choose internal representatives and the right to free action.

560. Such associations should be regulated by their own by-laws, and will be protected, the Act insists, against any infringement upon their freedom. By-laws have to have a certain minimum statutory content (name; trades and/or industry, and geographical jurisdiction; rules about their government and administration and their representative organs; economic resources; system of admission of members; and the regulations 'of their own functioning in agreement with democratic principles'). They are not subject to any formal approval or registration by any organ of the state although they shall deposit their by-laws in a public registry; the Registrar must publish in the Official State Bulletin an abstract of the by-laws and the association will be deemed to be legally incorporated and existing as a juridical person if, within a twenty-day period after the deposit of the abstract, there is no complaint about its legality (the Labour Court will decide on the legality if there is a complaint; the existence of any court decision on this matter has not come to our knowledge which means that there have been no complaints, although hundreds of abstracts about newly constituted workers' federations have been published).

561. The TUA insists on the employees' right to belong to trade unions on the sole condition of observing their by-laws. Trade unions can form any type of federation or confederation or affiliate themselves with anyone already in existence. They cannot be suspended or dissolved except by judicial proceedings based on serious violations of laws.

562. Employees, besides the right to join the union of their own choosing, are assured that they will be protected against any act of discrimination that, in relation to their employment, negates or tends to negate their trade union freedom. As we have seen above (Part I, Chapter 7, §6(I)) the WSA declares null and void employer's unilateral decisions that display unfavourable discrimination by reason of union membership or participation in union activities. Article 12 of the TUA insists on this point.

563. It is discriminatory to make it a condition of the labour contract not to belong to a certain trade union or to a union generally, and it is forbidden. A condition to enforce union membership in a contract is also discriminatory. Thus 'yellow dog' or closed shop contractual clauses come under this prohibition, as do the milder union shop or maintenance of membership type clauses.

564. Every employee or union can complain against any infringement of trade union freedom; and this through a special summary proceeding before Labour or ordinary courts. As we have seen (Introduction Chapter 5, 1, I), there is also a special protection appeal before the Constitutional Court (recurso de amparo), trade union freedom being one of the fundamental rights established in the Constitution.

565. The Constitution says that the internal structure and functioning of trade unions 'must be democratic'; a reference to this matter is also made, as we have seen, in the 1985 Act. The requirement is difficult to define, although it means at the least, free election for union offices, that the most important decisions are made at the Assembly or Congress, and that there is free expression and deliberation.

566. The TUA establishes a special type of union, the 'more representative union' and confers on it a special position for the purposes of representative action. Two kinds of this type of union are regulated: (a) the more representative union at national level: unions that have obtained at least 10% of the members of the representative institutions of the employees in work centres (shop stewards and work centre councils, as we shall see later, Chapter 2) of the whole national territory; (b) the more representative union at autonomous region level: unions that have obtained at least 15% of the members of these representative organs in a regional territory, with a minimum of 1,500 members.

To these unions the law recognizes a series of important faculties which other unions do not have; some of these faculties are discussed below.

567. The TUA refers also to unions which have obtained at least 10% of the members of representative organs in work centres, not at national or regional level, but at a determined territorial and industry level (in banking or in transport, for example); these 'representative unions' in a lower scope also have representative functions, but less than the more representative ones.

568. The Constitution reserves the expression 'trade union freedom', as we have seen, to the freedom of the employees to form unions and to belong to them. The Act 19/1977 mentioned above, however, referred to employees' unions and to employers' associations. However, the TUA applies only to the first ones and maintains the application of the 1977 Act to the second ones. This means that employees' unions and employers' associations are regulated by different Acts, the first by the TUA and the second by the 1977 Act.

569. In addition to this, we must say that the Constitutional Court has repeatedly said that 'union freedom' applies only to employees; in other words, freedom of association of employers is placed outside trade union freedom.

§3. The Experience of Trade Union Freedom

570. As we have said, the TUA establishes that an abstract of a registered by-law shall be published in the Official State Bulletin. Anyone interested can impugn the legality of the union and a proceeding before the Labour Court opens as a result of the claim. Twenty days after the deposit of the by-laws (or after the sentence of the Court, in this case) the union is a legal person.

571. Almost as soon as the executive regulations of the 1977 Act were published, there was, it seems, a rush of associations presenting their by-laws to the

Registrar. The Official State Bulletin has published the abstracts of literally hundreds of by-laws, corresponding to other employees' and employers' associations.

It is clear that the beginning of trade union freedom was followed by a high degree of pluralism. It must be said, however, that most of these associations have very little or no activity, with a very low number of members; certain of these have even dissolved. As happens in other countries, only a small number of these associations – as we shall see later – really accomplish any true activity in the labour relations system, representing significant groups of employees and employers.

572. Both employers and employees use quite a variety of general names for their unions: confederation, federation, association, society, guild, community, centre, 'sindicato' (which in Spain means union) and 'unión' (which in Spanish is a generic word which means vague association). Except perhaps for 'confederación', which tends to mean a union with unions, not individuals, as members, the other titles have no fixed meaning at all.

573. The most important Employees' Confederations are the Confederación Sindical de Comisiones Obreras (CC.OO.) and the Unión General de Trabajadores (UGT). As far as members' numbers go, minor federations are the Unión Sindical Obrera (USO), the Central Sindical Independiente y de Funcionarios (CSIF), the Confederación General del Trabajo (CGT) and the Confederación Nacional del Trabajo (CNT). All of them are 'national' and all of them say that they are open to any type of worker, or to any workers' unions. There are several confederations of regional scope; among them, we must mention the Solidaridad de Trabajadores Vascos (ELA-STV) and the Confederación Sindical Gallega (CIG), unions with important membership, respectively, in the Basque and Galician regions.

574. There are no official statistics on the number of members in every trade union. Confederations provide few facts on this matter and it seems these are not very reliable. It is certain that, after the recovery of trade union freedom in 1977 there was an important membership movement on the employees' side, followed by a certain reflux. The causes of this reflux are different to state. The fact that collective agreements normally have, as we shall see later (Chapter 3), normative effects for every employee (unionized or non-unionized) included in the bargaining unit is probably one of the most important. The lower union conscience of many employees and the difficulties of employment since the early 1970s have had a negative effect on the entire labour relations system.

575. Although membership rates can be low, some recent studies show that 'union influence', i.e., the influence of unions on the whole working class and its support of union activity, is maintained at a higher rate. The only official rate to measure this influence is the result of the elections for employees' representatives in the enterprise: more than 30% of the elected representatives belong to CC.OO., and a similar number belong to UGT. The rest belong to smaller unions or are 'independent' employees, meaning that non-unionized employees.

576. Trade union freedom guaranteed by the Constitution includes, of course, freedom to organize; every Confederation can structure itself according to its own interests. There is, however, a generally recognized and adopted pattern: a 'horizontal' structure, the 'unión' exists in every province for all the employees of this territorial circumscription, whatever branch they may be employed in. The national 'federación' groups the employees in every branch of industry, services and agriculture, sometimes national federations by crafts or of retired employees. The 'confederación' is the superior organization which comprises all the inferior structures, horizontal and vertical.

577. The organs of the Confederation are also similar in general: the 'Congreso', which is formed by representatives from every affiliated organization and assembled every two or three years, is the supreme deliberating and decision-making organ. The 'Comité ejecutivo' carries through the daily government of the Confederation. A 'Comité confederal' or similar, restricted assembly assumes the higher direction and representation between Congresses.

578. The practice of freedom of association by employers has led also to a certain pluralism of organizations, although only a few of them can pretend to represent a significant sector of employers. The dominant organization is indeed the Confederación Española de Organizaciones Empresariales (CEOE) which groups territorial and branch organizations of industry, services and agriculture. The Confederación Española de la Pequeña y Mediana Empresa (CEPYME) aspires to represent the greater number of little and median employers and is today federated in the CEOE. Other employers' associations indeed exist, but their number of members seems rather lower.

579. These employers' associations group organizations of more restricted scope, either territorial (that is, open to any employer of the same province or region) or of a branch (open to any employer of a determined sector of the economy). Thus, as in other countries, Spanish employers' associations structure themselves in a shape similar to employees' trade unions.

580. Needless to say, at every geographical level, and in every important sector of industry, there are several employers' and employees' associations which presumably compete, without clear jurisdictional or demarcation lines, for the same potential membership. Besides, abstracts have been published of associations whose membership cannot possibly be made up of employers or employees. As has been said, and this is not the only case, there are some federations for retired employees; there are also associations of artisans or independent workers; and there are associations of farmers who with their families, cultivate their own land; and several employers' and employees' associations are open to these types of membership.

§4. The Unionization of Public Employees

581. The Constitution guarantees the right of everyone to unionize freely and adds: 'the law can exclude or limit the exercise of their right to unionize for military personnel and shall regulate peculiarities of this exercise for public employees'. That means that (with the possible exceptions) public employees can form unions and belong to them, as all other employees; their peculiarities cannot affect their basic rights.

582. In accordance with the Constitution, Article 1 of the TUA excludes military personnel from its regulation. The Royal Ordinances of Armed Forces (Royal Decree 96/2009, of 6 February) confirms the absence of the right to unionize for military personnel.

583. The TUA says that the right of civil police personnel belonging to unionize – non-military personnel therefore – shall be regulated by specific rules. An Act of 13 March 1986 and some executive rules establish the peculiarities in the exercise of this right, mainly the complete independence of these unions from other employees' unions.

584. The Constitution expressly forbids judges and state attorneys to affiliate to a union. The organic rules of these two special groups of public employees confirm the prohibition, allowing for the creation of professional associations for the defence of their interests of a non-unionized nature.

585. The public employees' unions are covered by the TUA rules, as are the unions of employees working for private employers. They can form federations and confederations and affiliate with those already existing, in both cases unionizing public and/or private employees.

586. The TUA forbids either general directors of the public administration or higher personnel from occupying high union offices.

Chapter 2. Institutionalized Relations Between Employers and Employees

§1. INTRODUCTION

587. Before 1977, a system of representation of employees in the enterprise was formed, through which the 'institutionalized relations' mainly took place. The present system of internal representation has some similarities with the old one although today's union freedom – which did not exist at all before 1977 – is a basic difference between them.

588. The basic structure – today regulated by the WSA – has two components, the shop stewards ('delegados de personal') and the enterprise or work centre council ('comité de empresa'). An institution regulated in the ES, which appears for the first time in Spanish labour law, is the employees' meeting in the work centre ('asamblea'), also a lesser component of the entire system.

Whether shop stewards or work centre council (actually a council of stewards) shall exist depends on the number of employees (*see* above in Chapter 1).

The LRPA gives rules on information and consultation rights of employees' representatives in safety and hygiene matters; more recently, an Act of 24 April 1997 regulates information and consultation rights in EU-scope enterprises. Notice of both matters must also be given.

§2. SHOP STEWARDS

589. Shop stewards are elected in every enterprise or workshop of more than ten and less than fifty employees; on work sites of more than six employees and less than ten, a shop steward is elected if the majority of the personnel desires to have this representation.

Where there are up to thirty employees in the enterprise or work site, a shop steward is elected; if there are more than thirty employees and less than fifty (which is the higher limit, as we have said) three shop stewards are elected.

590. Shop stewards are elected for a four-year period; re-election is always legally possible. Electors are all the employees of the enterprise and eligible as candidates are those nominated by the trade unions or by a number of employees of the enterprise that at least represent three times the number of shop stewards to be elected. Candidates should be more than 18 years of age and employed in the enterprise with a seniority of at least six months.

591. The WSA says that shop stewards have 'the representation of the employees of the enterprise or work site'. They should exercise their representative office jointly, in the case of there being several representatives.

592. Shop stewards, acting alone or as a body, are the representatives of the employees in dealing with the employer and his representatives about the one thousand-and-one questions immediately emerging from the place and time of work, where and when 'labour conditions' actually take place and are actually experienced by the employees whom the shop stewards represent. What the shop steward does is interpose his representative authority between the employer and the employees represented by him, when the latter believe that their rights and interests are infringed by the former's orders or decisions in the working situation. The WSA states that they have the same functions as that of the work centre council and they are discussed below (§3, III).

593. In the case where the collective bargaining unit is the enterprise or the work centre (as we will see in Chapter 3) and either of them has an employees' council, the shop stewards, or some of their number chosen by them, are the parties with the representation for collective bargaining purposes.

594. Shop stewards have a special protection system in order to carry out their representative function. The guarantees established by the law refer both to the protection against a certain conduct of the employer; and to facilities to make compatible their work as employees and their representative office. Those guarantees are the same for shop stewards and for members of the work council; we will see them in §3.

§3. Enterprise or Work Centre Council

595. The WSA defines work centre council as 'the representative and collegiate organ of the personnel of the enterprise for the defence of their interests'. It is, again in the words of the WSA, the organ through which employees participate in the enterprise. Is one of the types of employees' participation in the enterprise which Article 129 of the Constitution charges the public powers to promote.

I. Structure

596. The basis for the establishment of a council is not the enterprise but the work centre. There shall be one council in every work centre which occupies fifty or more employees. Thus, if the enterprise has more than one work centre with fifty or more employees, one council must be elected in each. The law adds that if the enterprise has in the same province several centres, none of them with fifty employers but the total sum reaches fifty, there shall be a 'conjoint council', the only one for all these work centres. The general concept of work centre for the ES is 'the production unit with a specific organization'.

597. In an enterprise with more than one work centre which occupies fifty or more employees each, it is possible to form an 'inter-work centre council', in addition to the others. This council can be created only through a collective agreement.

The WSA gives only two additional rules: the number of the members of this special council cannot be more than thirteen, and these members are elected by the members of the work centre councils and from among themselves.

A certain number of enterprise collective agreements effectively create this inter-work centre council as a representative organ of all employees in the enterprise with information and consultation rights extended to common or general questions of every work centre.

598. The number of members of the work centre council is fixed by the WSA on a scale which begins at 5 members (work centres from 50 to 100 employees) and ends at 21 members (work centres from 751 to 1,000 employees), plus 2 additional members for every 1,000 additional employees or fraction. The council chooses a chairman and a secretary from among its members and writes its own by-laws.

II. Election

599. Employees' members of the work centre council are chosen for a four-year period and re-election is legally possible. As in the case of the shop stewards, electors are all the employees of the enterprise and eligible candidates are nominated by the trade unions or by a number of employees of the enterprise that at least represents three times the number of members to be elected. Candidates should be more than 18 years of age and employed in the enterprise with a seniority of at least six months.

600. The WSA regulates in detail the electoral proceeding, which can be presented here in a very synthetic way. The electoral body is divided into two electoral colleges: workers in the first one, technicians and clerks in the second one; a third college can be created by collective agreement when the distribution of the personnel makes it necessary. Every college chooses different members of the council, which are distributed among them according to their respective numbers.

601. In the normal case, there are different lists of candidates, each one containing a number of names equal to the number of members eligible; lists are presented by unions (more frequently) or by a group of employees at least three times the number of the council's members to be elected; one or other fact must be clearly mentioned. The elector can only vote for one of the lists.

602. Each list of candidates receives a number of places in the council according to a proportional system. Lists that do not obtain at least 5% of the votes receive no place in the council.

603. The WSA gives rules about the election board, its competences, the presentation of lists of candidates, vote proceedings, casting of votes and publication of results.

Claims on electoral matters are submitted to an arbitration proceeding that is regulated by the WSA and more specifically by a Royal Decree 1844/1994, of 9

September 1994. Arbitrators are nominated by unions for a five-year period. Their decisions may be appealed before the Labour Court according to a special proceeding.

604. Members of the work centre council (the same is applied to shop stewards) can be revoked before the end of their four-year mandate through a decision of the majority of the employees who chose them, in a meeting convoked with this object.

III. Functions

605. A new redaction of Article 64 WSA, introduced in 2007 (transposing an EU Directive), allows us to present the functions of the work centre council following three items: information rights, consultation rights and other functions. The same is applied to shop stewards, as was said above.

A. *Information Rights*

606. As we will see immediately, a characteristic point of the Spanish system of employees' representation in the enterprise is that its organs are at the same time subjects of collaboration with the employer, with different purposes, and agents of conflict with the same employer, acting as representative of opposite interests.

607. The following should be mentioned as the most important:

- The council should be informed at least once every three months by the employer about the current situation and future prospects of employment, production and sales of the enterprise. Presumably, the council may deliberate upon this information, giving its advice and/or proposing some measure on this basis.
- The council should have at its disposal the balance sheet and the same documents as the shareholders are entitled to (if the company is a corporation).
- It must be informed of the employer's previsions on new labour contracts, their number and categories, including part-time contracts.
- The council should be informed about absenteeism, work-connected accidents and professional illness statistics; and also, about sanctions imposed by the employer in the case of serious faults.
- At least once yearly it must receive information from the employer about application in the enterprise of equality rights between women and men, namely measures to improve it and the application of the 'equality plan' in the enterprise when it exists.
- Likewise, the council must be informed by the employer of the action measures planned for the activation of alerts for catastrophes and other adverse meteorological phenomena.
- Finally, receive the basic copy of all labour contracts, as well as notification of extensions and terminations corresponding to them.

Article 64 WSA obliges the employer to provide the information to the employees' representatives in due time and with correct content, in order to allow them full knowledge and make proposals, where necessary, in their report.

B. Consultation Rights

608. There is a whole series of these included in the WSA, the most important ones being:

- On any proceeding for total or partial lay-offs due to technological or economic causes (as stated in Part I, Chapter 6, §1(II)), the council can negotiate an agreement with the employer on the solution of the crisis situation. In any case, it must report on the situation that provokes those layoffs.
- The council should report on work-time reductions, transfers of the work centre, professional training plans, piece-work rates and productivity bonuses, control of productivity systems, etc.
- The council should report any complaint of the employee about his professional classification within the enterprise; over flexible working hours; and payment of wages by cheque or bank transfer.

609. Consultation by the employer must be made at an appropriate time and with the correct content, in order to allow the employees' representatives to meet with the employer, to obtain his reasoned answer and – if this is the case – obtain an agreement with him. The report of the council must be provided in a maximum of fifteen days.

C. Other Functions

610. The WSA adds other different functions of the employees' representatives:

- to watch over the performance by the employer of labour, social security and employment laws; the council can initiate legal proceedings before the employer and before administrative and jurisdictional organs;
- to watch over conditions of security and health of work in the enterprise and over application of equality of treatment between women and men;
- to participate in the direction of the enterprise's social facilities;
- to collaborate with the employer on sustenance and improvement of productivity in the enterprise. This is a very extensive function, referring to very different subjects of the enterprise and employees' activity;
- to inform employees of the enterprise about the subjects of its own jurisdiction, if they affect the enterprise's labour relations;
- as we will see (below Chapter 3, §3), the council negotiates collective agreements in employer and work centre bargaining units. Needless to say, this really adds a discussion of conflicting interests to the conception of the council as an organ of cooperation;

– the council bargains with the employer on modification of essential conditions of work proposed by the latter; and on transfer of employees from one to another work centre of the same enterprise.

611. Since 1994 the law has considerably extended the cases of bargaining between employer and employees' representatives. Generally speaking, those changes look forward to obtaining a higher level of flexibility on conditions of work in the enterprise, adapting these conditions to the changing economic and employment circumstances. The extended possibilities offered to these agreements between the two parties mostly suppose a consequent restriction or limitation of the law on regulating the affected conditions of work.

612. The results which can be attributed to the council's intervention, or lack of it, in the previously mentioned matters obviously differ from one to another. In the cases where an agreement between the council and the employer is required, obviously, the agreement does not exist without the presence of the council. When a previous report is required, a general rule must be the nullity of the decision which is taken without it. When a report to the council is obligatory and the employer does not provide one, there is an infraction and the administration can sanction the employer.

613. The mentioned modification of Article 64 WSA (following also in this point the EU Directive) asks the employer and the work centre council to act in their information and consultation functions in a 'spirit of cooperation', taking into consideration both the enterprise's and employees' interests.

IV. Proceedings

614. The council writes up its procedure rules, where there are specifications about the calling of meetings, deliberations and resolutions. A chairman and a secretary are elected from among its members.

615. The council must hold an ordinary meeting once every two months and as many extra meetings as needed, provided the meetings are called by one-third of its members or by one-third of the employees. The employer must put at the service of the council an adequate place in the work centre for its normal activities and the best communication between the representatives and the employees.

V. Guarantees and Facilities

616. Members of the council – and shop stewards – have a special statute for protection of their delicate position as employees' representatives. This statute includes guarantees regarding the employer's behaviour and facilities for a better performance of their functions.

617. Among the guarantees, the employee cannot be dismissed or sanctioned because of his legal activities as such a representative during the four-year mandate and up to one year afterwards. In the case of common, serious breaches of the labour contract, the employer must follow a 'contradictory proceeding', with the hearing of the employee himself and of the rest of the representatives.

618. In addition to this, the law expressly forbids discriminatory decisions of the employer on remuneration or professional advancement of the employee because of his representative functions. The employee has the right to express freely his opinions about the matters concerning these functions; decisions of the Constitutional Court have conditioned this right to the basic employer interests, the veracity of the information and the bona fides principle.

619. Among the privileges, every member of the council disposes of a number of hours every month, to exercise the function of his representation: the WSA fixes a scale which begins at fifteen hours in work centres or enterprises with fewer than 100 employees and ends at forty hours in work centres or enterprises with more than 250 employees.

This number of hours is remunerated and can be accumulated by collective agreement on one or more of the representatives.

In addition to the adequate place which must be put, by the employer, at the disposal of the council, a notice board must also be put at its service for communications to the personnel.

620. Members of the council and shop stewards have a preferential right to stay as employees of the enterprise with regard to other employees in case of termination or suspension of their contracts due to technological or economic causes.

621. The WSA fixes an important limit to the representative office: shop stewards and members of the work centre council have a duty of secrecy on reserved information provided by the employer, and this is for the full four-year mandate and after it.

§4. Representatives on Safety and Health Matters

622. As stated in Part I, Chapter 2, §3(I), the LRPA gives some important rules on information and consultation rights of employees' representatives in the enterprise on safety and hygiene matters.

623. Shop stewards and members of the work centre council choose between themselves a number of representatives with specific functions on the matter ('delegados de prevención'). The employer must consult them on conditions of work, health and safety matters; and they have a right to watch over the effective application of prevention rules in the enterprise.

A collective agreement can establish a different system of designation, provided the authority to designate belongs to the employees' representatives or to employees directly.

624. A council on safety and health ('Comité de seguridad y salud') must be created in every work centre with fifty or more employees. This specific council is integrated by the 'delegados de prevención' and by the same number of employer representatives. Its functions cover the ordinary and periodical consultation by the employer on health and safety matters. It has also faculties on planning and application of prevention rules, the promotion of more effective means of prevention, and receiving from the employer the necessary information.

§5. Work Centre Meetings

625. The WSA includes the right of the employees to meet in an assembly in the work centre premises. This meeting is a means of direct expression of the collective will of the employees and a means for their direct information.

626. The meeting can be called (once every two months and outside working time) by shop stewards, the work centre council or a number of employees amounting to not less than one-third of the personnel. Notification must be communicated to the employer. People not employed in the enterprise may be present, what probably refers to union representatives.

627. The law says nothing about the specific competence of the assembly, except in two cases: we have seen the first one, revocation of shop stewards or members of the work centre council; the other is to inform employees about collective bargaining. As we have said, the assembly is a means of direct expression of the collective will of the employees, a deciding organ. The WSA requires, for resolution of the assembly which affects all employees, a positive vote of 50% plus one of the employees of the enterprise; through this rule, the law will prevent resolutions taken by a minority of employees.

628. Collective agreements frequently regulate assemblies in the work centre in a more favourable or complete way (for example, agreeing more frequent meetings or meetings in working time).

§6. Work Centre Union Representatives

629. The TUA establishes that employees' members of a union can create a union section ('sección sindical de empresa') in the enterprise or work centre. As union members, they can meet in assembly (meetings obviously different to these general meetings of employees, mentioned above), collect union fees and distribute union information.

630. Sections of the more representative unions and of the unions that have obtained at least one of the representative places of the work centre council have several additional advantages: a notice board for union communications to the personnel, an adequate place to fulfil its activities in the work centre, the right to collective bargaining at plant or enterprise level.

631. In work centres with more than 250 employees, the union sections of the unions that have obtained at least one of the representative places of the work centre council can appoint a 'union delegate' ('delegado sindical'), actually a new type of shop steward, with representative functions. Up to four of these delegates can be appointed in work centres with a higher number of employees.

632. Union delegates must receive from the employer the same information as the work centre council and shop stewards; they have the right to sit without a vote in work centre council meetings; they shall report in the case of employer's collective measures that touch employees' interests, especially when these ones are members of the union.

633. Union delegates are not affected by the 'cooperation duty' with regard to the employer, as work centre council members and shop stewards are, as we have seen above. This is an important difference between the information and consultation functions of both representatives.

634. Union delegates have the same guarantees as shop stewards and members of the work centre council. They have the same duty of secrecy.

§7. Direct Representation of Interests of Workers Themselves

635. The direct representation of the interests of workers themselves is a legal option that was incorporated into Spanish Law a few years ago. Initially, it was considered a possibility, in cases where the company intends to make substantial modifications to the working conditions, of a collective nature, or collective dismissals, and which according to Spanish regulations must be negotiated, in principle, with the unitary representatives or workers' unions. Specifically, what the legal norm establishes is that, in the event that there is no legal representation of the workers in the workplace, they may choose to attribute their representation for the negotiation of the agreement, at their choice, to a commission of a maximum of three members, made up of workers from the company itself and democratically elected by them, or a commission of an equal number of components designated, according to their representativeness, by the most representative unions of the sector to which the company belongs, and that were legitimized to be part of the negotiating committee of the collective agreement applicable to it.

636. However, this is a formula that has not worked correctly in practice. In fact, and subsequently, in relation to other matters, for example, in the case of the negotiation of equality plans, the legal formula that has been chosen, when there is no legal representation of the workers, is to directly recognize the representative capacity of the workers' unions that are more representative and representative of the sector to which the company belongs, and with legitimacy to be part of the negotiating committee of the applicable collective agreement, ruling out the possibility that workers can represent themselves directly.

§8. Representatives of Employees on the Board of Directors of Business Corporations

637. These union delegates co-exist with shop stewards and work centre councils in a certain number of enterprises or work centres, these of a higher number of employees, where unions can create union sections. The distribution of functions between these two types of representatives of employees is not always decided by the law in a very clear way, which probably means that the decision on which of them will actually act is merely a practical one.

638. Generally speaking under Spanish mercantile and corporation law, the governing of a corporation – which adopts the form of a joint stock company, 'sociedad anónima' – is entrusted by the shareholders to a board of directors ('consejo de administración') which has all the powers of the corporation subject only to the approval of, and review by, the yearly shareholders meeting. Apart from approving the annual board report, only topics such as an important change in the business of the corporation or its dissolution, the reduction or increase of the previously approved number of shares, or modification of the by-laws are subject to decision by the shareholders' meeting.

639. In 1962, the law established 'the participation of personnel in the administration of enterprises which were legally corporations' and had other requisites.

There should be one employee representative on the board for every six other board members, a minority representation therefore. In practice, this representative had little importance.

640. The WSA has abolished the Act which regulated this special type of representation of the employees, and has established no similar one. No new regulation on this matter is likely at this time.

641. In 1986 and 1993 two agreements between the most representative unions and representatives of state administration were reached; among other things, a representation of unions in the board of directors of corporations shared by the state was established.

642. Although, as we have said, there is not a general provision on this matter, certain branches know a specific regulation. This is the case with saving banks and cooperatives, where respectively two Acts of 1985 and 1999 have introduced employees' representatives on the direction boards.

§9. Information and Consultation Rights in EU-Wide Enterprises

643. The Act 10/1997 of 24 April has transposed into Spanish labour law EU Directive of 22 September 1994 on information and consultation rights in EU-wide enterprises and a group of enterprises.

EU-wide enterprises are enterprises with at least 1,000 employees in the EU, with at least 150 employees in two Member States. EU-wide groups of enterprises are groups with at least 1,000 employees in the EU with at least two enterprises in different Member States with at least 150 employees each.[7] This Act was amended by Act 10/2011, transposing into Spanish law the Directive 2009/38/EC, of 6 May.

644. The central board of the enterprise or group, when it is in Spain, is obliged to open a bargaining proceeding with the employees' representatives in order to establish a 'European work centre council' or, alternatively, an employees' information and consultation proceeding on transnational questions about employees' interests. If the central board rejects the bargaining or an agreement is not reached within three years, the establishment of a European work centre council becomes obligatory. The law has rules about its organization and functions.

645. The law also regulates the number and designation system of employees' representatives in enterprises and groups of enterprises with their central board in a different Member State of the EU. In principle, these representatives are designated among the shop stewards, members of the work centre council and work centre union representatives (existing in Spanish enterprises, as we have seen in Chapters §2, 3, and 6).

646. These employees' representatives at the European level have the same guarantees as the 'national' ones (*see* above in this chapter, §3.V) and some additional hours yearly to exercise their special representation.

647. Directive 2001/26 on the involvement of employees in the European Corporation, and Directive 2003/72 on the involvement of employees in the European Cooperative, have been transposed into Spanish labour law by Act 31/2006 of 18 October. This regulation is similar to Act 10/1997 on information and consultation rights in EU-wide enterprises and groups of enterprises.

7. On this subject can be found a comprehensive study: F. Elorza Guerrero, *European Works Council Spain*, in *Labour Law and Industrial Relations*, Kluwer Law International BV, 2025.

Chapter 3. Collective Bargaining

§1. Introduction

648. 'Collective bargaining' is an expression which in normal and legal use comprises both negotiating activity with a view to obtaining a set of rules collectively agreed between employer and employees for the regulation of labour conditions, as well as the collective agreements themselves. This applies entirely to Spanish labour law. Its basic regulation is contained today in the WSA, which regulates the proceedings of collective bargaining and the agreement which is the result of the bargaining.

649. From the point of view of Spanish labour law the trade agreement is formally recognized as a source of law, not a simple or gentlemen's private agreement; the trade agreement impinges upon labour conditions from outside as any enactment does, and not from the inside, as a part of the labour contract or relationship. In this situation there is no need to use an esoteric or anachronistic theory about the 'incorporation' in the labour contract of the clauses of the trade agreement; naturally, so to speak, the former comes under the latter and is regulated by it, as by any other source of law; and as law it will be treated by the courts; the problems about how to place the trade agreement within the hierarchy of sources of law have already been discussed (*see* Introduction, Chapter 5, §§7 and 10).

650. The WSA has abolished the Collective Bargaining Act of 1973 which for its part had abolished another Act of the same name enacted in 1958. This Act of 1958 had reintroduced in Spain the establishment of labour conditions through collective bargaining, after a period of more than twenty years in which trade agreements were formally and legally unknown, although a certain amount of informal – illegal, if you wish – collective bargaining went on within the enterprises, especially about wages and remuneration. Before the Civil War, the collective bargaining system was less than well developed; although some of it existed, most of the labour conditions were fixed by semi-public bodies in which, of course, employers and employees were represented, but whose chairmanship belonged to an impartial, Government-appointed, official. In 1942, even this system was formally abolished and a network of labour ordinances gradually appeared in lieu of it. It was upon this network that the Collective Bargaining Act of 1958, and later on the Act of 1973, were superimposed, making for a complex situation: collective agreements bargained in the application of 1958 and 1973 Acts lived together with labour ordinances. As we have seen (Introduction, Chapter 5, §4), today the situation is much clearer since labour ordinances have been derogated.

651. Between 2010 and 2012 some important items of collective bargaining have been modified, promoting more flexibility. Before these legal reforms, the collective agreement had been applied as a general rule but after these measures, a preference for the enterprise agreement has been declared. The aim is to favour the adaptation of conditions of work to the requirements of enterprises in certain matters: working time, distribution of hours of work, work by shifts, modalities of remuneration, rates of wages, remuneration by result, functions (when they exceed the limits of their modification authorized by the law) and free increases in social security benefits. Additionally, some legal means have been provided in order to ensure that bargaining proceedings without a result may be resolved by mediation or arbitration: this will make possible adaptation of the conditions of work to the changing economic circumstances.

652. However, at the end of 2021, a legislative reform was approved that, finally, led to a repeal of some of the regulations approved in 2012, thereby restoring certain approaches that had been in force in our country for years. More specifically, the 2021 labour reform, and with regard to collective bargaining, once again legally recognized that collective agreements could remain in force (extended validity) as long as the negotiation of the new agreement was taking place. Likewise, it eliminated the legal recognition of the application priority of company agreements regarding salaries.

§2. Collective Bargaining Units

653. The WSA does not establish a list of collective bargaining units. As a general regulation says that 'collective agreements shall have the scope of application that the parties decide'; implicitly, it must be understood that this scope coincides with the representation scope of the parties.

654. From the regulation of the WSA we can deduce, however, that the following bargaining units are legally possible:

- a unit lower than the enterprise as an economic unity; this can be, in the first place, a work centre with a specific, autonomous organization; a section or department, also with special characteristics within the organization of the enterprise; lastly, a group of employees defined by their professional classification;
- a single enterprise, whether it has one or more work centres, either in the same or in several localities or provinces;
- all the enterprises within the same economic branch (banking, chemical industry, for example) or a more specific section (road transport, travel agencies, for example). According to the territorial coverage of each of these branches or sections, there are several possibilities: so, a collective agreement can be bargained for all the enterprises of the same branch in the province, in the region or in the entire national territory;
- all companies that are members of a business group; also, a plurality of companies linked for organizational or productive reasons.

655. The WSA extends these cases of bargaining units to another two cases. The first is the so-called inter-professional agreements, whose purpose is not the direct regulation of conditions of work applicable to individual labour relations, but regulation of the collective bargaining itself (bargaining units, conflicts between the coverage of different agreements, settlement of different bargaining units, etc.). The second case is the 'inter-sectoral collective agreements', which should regulate directly conditions of work as the agreements which are the result of each one of the three bargaining units mentioned above, but with a scope enlarged to several branches. The WSA requires that the two types mentioned here shall be bargained by the most representative unions and employers' associations.

656. In any case, Spanish law establishes a series of rules to resolve the problems that may arise from the concurrence over time of collective agreements negotiated in different bargaining units, such as:

- Respect for the validity of the collective agreement in force, which may not be affected by the provisions of collective agreements of different scope, unless so provided by an interprofessional agreement.
- The application priority, with respect to the working conditions established in sectoral collective agreements, of certain conditions established in company agreements (also in collective agreements for a group of undertakings or a plurality of undertakings), specifically: the payment or compensation of overtime and the specific remuneration for shift work; the schedule and distribution of working time, the shift work regime and annual vacation planning; the adaptation to the scope of the undertaking of the professional classification system of workers; the adaptation of the aspects of the contracting modalities that are attributed by this law to undertaking agreements; measures to promote co-responsibility and reconciliation between work, family and personal life.
- The recognition that collective agreements and interprofessional agreements at the Autonomous Community level (Spanish Autonomous Region) will have application priority over any sectoral collective agreement or agreement at the State level, provided that the negotiators meet certain requirements established in the WSA.
- The same application priority as in the previous case is recognized for provincial collective agreements, when it is established by an interprofessional agreement at the Autonomous Community level, and its content is more favourable than what is established in State agreements. However, this application priority is excluded in relation to the following matters, where a unitary conventional regulation is required: trial period; contracting modalities; professional classification; maximum annual working time; disciplinary regime; minimum standards on occupational risk prevention; and geographic mobility.

657. Within the bargaining units employees of both public and private sectors may be included and usually are – unless there is an employer unit – but this does not apply to employees with the status of public servants or with administrative-type contracts (but it should be added, the ILO Convention no. 84 ratified by Spain provides that the state has placed itself under an obligation to guarantee to its employees conditions of work no less favourable than the standard for the same type of work in the same region, including those collectively bargained).

658. Today's industrial relations system in Spain is covered by a large number of agreements, mainly of branches or sections and of enterprises. In recent years, branch agreements (national, regional and provincial) and also enterprise agreements have decreased in number as a consequence of the economic crisis and the closing of enterprises.

§3. The Parties to Collective Bargaining

659. The law distinguishes between an agreement bargained by an enterprise or an inferior unit and an agreement bargained by a superior unit.

If the bargaining unit is a work centre or an enterprise, the parties to the collective bargaining will be:

- on the employer's side, the employer himself or someone appointed by him to this effect;
- on the employees' side, the work centre council, shop stewards or the internal representation of the union in the enterprise; in the last case, it is necessary that these representations have the majority of the members of the work centre council if the agreement is going to be applied to the entire personnel of the enterprise. If the agreement is directed at a group of employees with a specific professional profile, the unions that have been designated by the majority of the employees by vote will be entitled to negotiate.

If the bargaining unit comprises enterprises of one branch or sector of the economy of any territorial level, the parties will be:

- on the employer's side, the employers' associations which affiliate at least 10% of all the employers (with at least 10% of the employees) in the bargaining unit;
- on the employees' side, the more representative unions and the unions which represent at least 10% of all the members of work centre councils or shop stewards in the bargaining unit.

In the case of agreements for a group of companies, as well as in agreements that affect a plurality of companies linked for organizational or productive reasons, the applicable rules to establish who can participate in these bargainings are the same as those established for sectorial bargaining

660. In the case of the multi-employer type of bargaining unit, the rules above establish only a minimum, non-sufficient legitimation. Bargaining proceedings can only be initiated legally – and agreements be legally reached – when the present employers' associations represent the majority of the employers of the bargaining unit; and when the unions or confederations represent the majority of members of work centre councils or shop stewards of the same unit.

§4. The Duty to Bargain and Actual Bargaining

661. Bargaining proceedings begin when one of the legitimated parties addresses the other in writing, inviting it to negotiate. The WSA requires the party which has taken the initiative to express the following points: the scope of its representation, coverage of the future agreement and the subjects it proposes to be negotiated.

662. The party which receives the invitation to bargain is not under a duty to reach an agreement but is under a duty to bargain and to do so in good faith with a view to reaching an agreement. This duty, however, has two important exceptions: when the initiative to negotiate tries to modify an agreement already in force and when there is a legal or bargained cause that hinders negotiation.

663. The parties must nominate the persons who are in the 'bargaining commission'. When the bargaining unit is sectoral, each party (employers/employees) may not name more than fifteen members; in any other case, each of the parties may not appoint more than thirteen members.

664. Bargaining itself is carried out by the representatives of the parties; agreements are adopted by a majority vote within each of the parties. The deliberation can be presided over by an impartial chairman with no direct or indirect interest in the matter; of course, the chairman has no vote, although his function is extremely important; more than one apparently impossible negotiation has been brought to a satisfactory ending by the good offices and expertise of the chairman. The parties may appoint advisers to present and defend their position.

665. At any point in the negotiation, the parties can agree upon the nomination of a mediator. The WSA gives no more rules about the proceeding in this case; it is clear that the mediator has no decision-making powers, he only tries to get the parties to reach an agreement.

666. The parties are under a duty to bargain in good faith, which of course excludes from the negotiation the use of any form of fraud, violence or coercion, which will make a contract invalid. Negotiation or its result (the agreement) is not invalid if during the bargaining proceedings there is friction or even conflict. However, the WSA declares the negotiation suspended immediately when there is violence against persons or goods and both parties verify this.

667. As to the number of meetings and their frequency there is neither any formal regulation, nor fixed practice; the negotiation goes on, smoothly or protractedly, until the parties have reached an agreement, or have acquired the conviction that an agreement is impossible and break the negotiation; these two possibilities must be studied separately.

I. If an Agreement Is Reached

668. To be valid, the agreement must be in writing. Within the next fifteen days, it must be sent to the administrative authority (Labour Ministry or autonomous region's labour administration, this second case if it has this faculty), which orders its registration and its deposit. The agreement is also sent for publication to the Official State Bulletin if the bargaining unit covers more than one province, or in the respective province bulletin. After its publication, the agreement becomes a source of labour law which shall be complied with and applied by the courts as needed.

669. When the administrative authority believes that the agreement infringes the law or violates a third party's rights, it communicates it to the Labour Court. This implies the beginning of a special proceeding, with a hearing of the parties to the agreement. The court shall declare the validity of the agreement or the total partial nullity of the agreement. If part of, or the entire agreement, is null, it is up to the parties to open new negotiations.

II. If an Agreement Is Not Reached

670. If the parties come to the conclusion that no agreement is possible there is then a situation of 'economic' or 'interest' dispute; its settlement will be discussed below (Chapter 5).

However, Spanish law establishes that during negotiations for the renewal of a collective agreement unless otherwise agreed, the collective agreement will remain in force, so that only the clauses of said agreement in which the right to strike had been waived, would lose validity, so it would be legal to call a strike precisely to put pressure on the negotiations.

In any case, the Spanish law also establishes that, after one year has elapsed since one of the parties expressed their desire not to continue extending the validity of the collective agreement, and an agreement on the new collective agreement has not been reached, the parties must submit to mediation procedures, which in some cases may also be arbitration, to resolve the unsuccessful completion of negotiations (we refer in this matter to the aforementioned Chapter V).

Finally, Spanish law is clear in establishing that, when the negotiation process has elapsed without reaching an agreement on the new collective agreement, the agreement in force until then will remain in force, as long as there is no new agreement unless the opposite is agreed by the negotiators.

§5. The Content of the Trade Agreement

671. We are now entering what is, a very complex and, at times, confusing topic of Spanish collective labour law. The plan we propose to follow will be to deal with the so-called obligatory content of the trade agreement and afterwards with its 'normative' content. Within the normative content, it will be necessary to distinguish further between, according to the WSA, a 'mandatory' content of the agreement which is mostly formed by norms that give the agreement its own peculiar structure (thereby the name usually given by scholars in Spain to this part: 'normas de configuración', configuration norms), and a non-mandatory content which actually contains the norms applicable to the labour relations of employers and employees included in the bargaining unit. And further, since not everything in every sense is open to collective bargaining, we will have to study first the legal limits of the trade agreement, and second, the possible content included within these limits. Lastly, we will pick up a thread which we left loose before, giving some notion about income policy measures and their impact on the contents of the trade agreement.

672. In any case, it must be remembered that, since the 2021 labour reform, the differentiation that had existed, in relation to the extended validity of the normative and obligatory contents of collective agreements, has disappeared. If prior to this labour reform, only the normative content (the obligatory ones, therefore, not) could see their validity extended, by the decision of the negotiators of the agreement, once the ordinary end date of the agreement had been reached, after the labour reform mentioned the extension of the validity, while a new collective agreement is negotiated, will affect all the clauses of the collective agreement, regardless of their normative or obligatory nature (the exception, as we have indicated in previous pages, are the clauses by which waiver of the strike, which will not be able to see its validity extended beyond the date scheduled for the collective agreement to cease to be in force).

673. Likewise, reference must be made to the progressive increase that, in recent years, has been registered in the set of matters required to be considered by collective agreements, and that we can identify as a content required by law (as 'contenido mínimo', (minimum content) is literally qualified by the law), always, of course, the law expressing that this is done assuming full respect of the parties to their freedom to negotiate. Thus, and together with traditional contents such as the determination of the parties that conclude the collective agreement, or the personal, functional, territorial and temporal scope, Article 85 WSA considers mandatory inclusion in every collective agreement aspect such as the procedures that can resolve the discrepancies that may arise in the negotiations to disapply the collective agreement within the framework of the procedure of Article 82.3 WSA, or the establishment of measures aimed at promoting equal treatment and opportunities between women and men in the workplace, or in their case the equality plans that certain companies must apply, and that also have to be negotiated. Likewise, the obligation to negotiate action protocols that contemplate risk prevention measures related to action against catastrophes and other adverse meteorological phenomena has also been included. If this minimum content is not in the collective agreement, it is not considered in accordance with the law.

I. Obligatory Content

674. The obligatory content is made up of the duties that the parties to the agreement accept towards each other; to generally comply with the agreement, to actually see in it a regulatory instrument, and not to indulge in any type of conduct, or allow their members to indulge in actions or conduct, which will impede the full strength of the agreement. In short, we have before us what is usually referred to as the peace duty derived from the trade agreement.

675. There is an implicit peace duty in every trade agreement; without going so far as to state the duty explicitly, the LRRDA says that 'no formal trade dispute is possible to modify the clauses of a trade agreement' (Article 20) and that a strike 'whose purpose is to alter the clauses of a trade agreement within the period in which it is in force' is an illegal strike (Article 11). Of course, these two rules must be understood in the simple sense that trade disputes – provided they are not disputes about the interpretation and application of the agreement itself – are forbidden, which means that the agreement is a peace treaty between the parties who do have a negative duty not to violate that agreement.

676. There can also be an explicit peace duty if the parties agree to it. Again, the LRRDA says that the trade agreement may contain: (a) rules about proceedings for the peaceful solution of disputes; and (b) the renunciation by the employees of their right to strike during the term of the agreement (Article 8). Presumably, both types of clauses will be adopted simultaneously and will be interrelated in the sense that it is hard to conceive the employees' renunciation of the right to strike if the agreement does not provide some way for the settlement of disputes. However, since during the term of the agreement only disputes about the interpretation and application of the agreement itself are possible, what this explicit peace duty consists of is the duty of the parties to continue the negotiation after the agreement to cover incidental matters pertaining to it and not clearly solved by it (*see* again below, Chapter 5, §2). The WSA confirms this rule in a certain sense when it says that 'collective agreements can regulate labour peace'.

677. In any case, it has to be borne in mind that, sometimes, certain clauses of a collective agreement may have a hybrid nature, in the sense that the same clause may coincide with mandatory and regulatory aspects. An example of this is the regulation of procedures to effectively resolve discrepancies that may arise in the negotiation to not apply certain aspects of the current collective agreement, within the framework of Article 82.3 WSA, referred to above. Well, in this specific case, while the commitment of the negotiators to resort to this extrajudicial settlement procedure has an obligatory nature between the negotiating parties, the regulation of the specific procedure, or the adaptation of another already existing in a settlement agreement scope is superior to the collective agreement itself, have a normative nature, since the result of the said procedure is projected on all the employees affected by the collective agreement.

II. Normative Content

678. Two types of clauses may be distinguished: configuration clauses and normative (proper) clauses.

A. Configuration of the Agreement

679. This type of clause gives the agreement, as was said before, its own peculiar structure. They are mandatory clauses which every agreement must contain; their main function is to make explicit the pre-existing bargaining unit, which now appears as the employees and employers whose labour relations are to be regulated by the agreement, and to give some idea of the agreement as a legal instrument. Better perhaps than this general description is to enumerate what these structural mandatory clauses are; according to Article 85 WSA, they are:

- the description of the parties that have reached the agreement, i.e., a clear reference to employer or employers' association, union, confederation or employees' representatives who subscribe to the agreement;
- the personnel, functional and geographical domain of the agreement, which means the ensemble of labour relationships regulated by it;
- the duration of the agreement, which the parties establish freely; the law does not impose a rigid term, minimum or maximum. If not otherwise established in the agreement itself, it comes into force on the date of its publication in the Official State Bulletin; but the parties may agree to a date of their own choosing, and they usually do so, perhaps making the agreement retroactive in whole or in part. If so the date must be settled expressly and clearly in a clause of the agreement. Two or three years duration is usual;
- the term within which the agreement must be denounced by either party, to avoid its extension to further yearly terms;
- the parties must provide for the establishment of one committee, formed by representatives of employers and employees, with specific functions related to the agreement; we will come back later to this important point.

B. Normative Clauses

680. The essence and the substance of the agreement, its very being, is in these clauses. They are normative in the sense that they will be applied to the labour contracts and relations between employers and employees included in the bargaining unit. The WSA leaves no doubt about this nature: it says that collective agreement is a 'source of regulation' of the labour relationships (Article 3).

681. As we have said at the beginning, we shall try to first outline the limits of the normative content, and second, the extension comprised within these limits.

1. The Limits of the Normative Content

682. The understanding of these limits is basic to the further understanding of all collective bargaining regulations of labour conditions. Roughly those limits are covered by the following four points:

a. Trade agreements are legally conceived as institutions to ameliorate labour conditions existing at the time of bargaining and so, a sensu contrario, an agreement establishing worse or no better conditions than those existing previously is not conceivable. However:
   - Conditions to be ameliorated are those contained in state norms. This means that customary conditions, and even conditions contained in previous trade agreements, are negotiable; Article 82.4 WSA says that the new agreement may dispose of the rights established in the old one. If there is an argument about the matter, to establish whether or not a trade agreement actually ameliorates the state norms, the comparison must be made 'in whole' – and not clause by clause, condition by condition – between the agreement and the pre-existing situation. If the agreement is 'better' as a whole, although it may not be so in some particular clause, that will be sufficient.
   - The law provides some leeway ('*descuelgue*') for enterprises in bad economic shape, and for what the parties actually agree about past conditions.
b. Conditions agreed upon in an individual labour contract by the employer and one employee – or more than one, of course, but contemplated singly – are intangible by the trade agreement, if they provide for better conditions for the particular employee. This is a firm rule – the maintaining of conditions ad personam – established by many decisions of the Labour Courts.
c. The system of collective bargaining is dominated by the vague but important idea that there are some basic conditions that cannot be touched upon, even if they appear externally to be favourable to any one, or both, of the parties concerned, or even if they do not appear so but are still purported to be part of an agreement which has some other clause or clauses making it more favourable 'as a whole'. Leaving aside obvious cases which appear clear enough to everyone concerned – the trade agreement cannot authorize labour contracts for life, or the employment of 10-year-old children no matter what are the 'favourable' conditions of the contract. Looking at a less apparently clear hypothesis, for instance, for the employer to entirely resign his right to discipline, because of wilful breaches of the contract of the employees – which the latter perhaps will find as favourable – is impossible; the employer can condone conduct and actions after the fact, but not beforehand, because the renunciation will be against the very basis of contractual law, leaving one party at the mercy of the others. For instance, again, it may seem favourable to the employer and even to the employees already within the bargaining unit, especially if it is a single employer or work-centre bargaining unit, to obtain a substantial wage increase or reduction of hours of work, giving as compensation to the employer a prolongation of the trial period of future employees; the clause will be, and actually has been already declared null and void as against public policy, which does

not allow for trials for more than reasonable periods of time, and which constructs any unreasonable prolongation, even if collectively agreed upon, as allowing the employer, again against public policy, which will amount to a contractual right to dismiss without proper cause.

d. The WSA forbids agreements that violate third persons' rights, i.e., persons not included in the bargaining unit. As we have seen, in this case, the administrative authority sends the agreement to the Labour Court, which will declare the validity or nullity of the agreement.

683. In some cases the freedom of the parties to bargain wages can be limited through income party rules, which try to reach a harmonic growth of the different incomes, prices and rents. In the past system, prior to the Constitution, successive rules (in 1967, 1969, 1973, 1975, 1977 and 1978) established limits to the wages that could be fixed by collective bargaining. Today, income policy regulation tends to obtain support from unions and employers' associations: thus, the last agreement signed, in this case between the unions CC.OO and UGT, and the employers' association CEOE-CEPYME (V Agreement for Employment and Collective Bargaining, 2024), contemplates a salary increase of 4% in 2023, and 3% in 2024 and 2025; as well as a 1% revision clause based on inflation.

2. The Normative Content

684. Within the limits just explained, the content of the collective agreement can extend to any type of labour conditions; using the expression of Article 85 WSA 'the agreement can regulate questions of economic, labour, collective and welfare matters, questions of employment in general, and relations between employees or their representative organizations and the employer and their associations'.

685. Taking a look at the several thousands of trade agreements in force, there can be found among them agreements which cover almost every conceivable labour condition, with a bettering of some or all of the previous conditions; and there can also be found very brief agreements, even with a single clause, providing, for instance, for a wage increase, either by a percentage or for a fixed amount in euros (this latter is the so-called lineal wage increase whose net effect, of course, is to reduce wage differentials) for all types of personnel included in the bargaining unit. And between those two extreme cases, a whole gamut of variants can be found. Perhaps if on one occasion a big effort was successfully made to reach a fairly comprehensive and detailed agreement, those immediately following would be much shorter.

686. Having said that, we must remember here that certain matters or conditions of work attract more attention than others from the agreement's parties. This is the case with remuneration, with a very detailed regulation about types of wages, benefits and bonuses, payment of overtime and seniority, profit-sharing and so on; also the case of working time (hours of work per day, week or year, overtime, hours of rest, holidays, annual vacation, etc.); classification of the employee according to his skill; methods of advancement following knowledges, merits and seniority; rules about a more safe place of work, adapted to the peculiarities of the branch or the enterprise, completing the LRPA norms, are also today very frequent, especially in activities with more serious risks.

687. Provision of social security benefits is part of the usual content of the trade agreement; since the protection generally provided by the 1994 Social Security Act is expressly stated as a minimum – the same expression appeared in the previous Social Security Acts of 1966 and 1974 – and the Act also explicitly says that these benefits may be improved through collective bargaining, employers and employees especially after 1966, entered into this domain with gladly. We may say that the recent collective bargaining continues along this line.

688. Miscellaneous benefits such as the direct provision of housing by the employer, or credits to buy a house, nurseries for children of female employees, and scholarships for employees or their dependants, are not infrequently included.

689. Special attention is dedicated to collective questions. In today's collective bargaining, we can observe an increasing interest in these questions, especially in the enlargement and improvement of the faculties, functions and protective measures of the representative organs in the enterprise: shop stewards, work centre council, unions' representatives; work centre meetings; and settlement of industrial disputes.

690. Application of the normative content of the agreement may be 'articulated', i.e., clauses negotiated in the enterprise are complementary to these bargained at the branch level; both agreements be applicable simultaneously. This solution, legally possible, is not very common in Spanish collective bargaining, the parties preferring on the contrary 'closed' agreements.

§6. Extension of the Collective Agreement

691. The Spanish collective labour law terminology distinguishes 'extensión' (extension of) and 'adhesión' (adhesion to) a collective agreement. Let us treat these two topics successively and separately.

692. The WSA provides that the Ministry of Labour may extend the provisions of a trade agreement to employers and employees not included in the bargaining unit, provided that 'there are special difficulties to collective bargaining' or 'significant circumstances of social or economic import' in that instance. Previously to the administrative decision, a committee formed by representatives of the most representative employers' associations and unions shall report over the extension itself.

693. The WSA further provides that the parties legitimated to bargain a collective agreement can decide not to agree on a new one but to adhere to another to which they have not been the negotiating parties. Adhesion requires that they are not obliged to a previous agreement; besides, it must be communicated to the administrative authority, in order to register the agreement: it is properly a collective agreement, although of a special type.

§7. The Interpretation of the Collective Agreement

694. We will examine this topic, starting first with the power to interpret a trade agreement, and the rules that preside over the interpretation.

I. The Power to Interpret

695. A legal and abstractly clear distinction is made by the WSA between a general interpretation and a particular or case-by-case interpretation.

696. The so-called general interpretation is assigned by the WSA to the Labour Courts. About a general interpretation, as opposed to a particular one, it may be said that it is an interpretation whose need is felt before an actual conflicting case develops, or at least before it has been formally submitted to any type of arbitration or court proceedings for decision. It should be added that, in the past, court decisions about this interpretation have been very pointed in saying that the power is a power to interpret, not a power to amend or modify the trade agreement. We can add that this interpretative function coincides with the Labour Courts' function to decide on collective disputes about the application of laws, in this case about the application of a collective agreement (as we have seen in Part I, Chapter 10, 1 and 3(II)(A)).

697. As we have seen above, the parties of the trade agreement must nominate a committee formed by representatives of employers and employees ('comisión paritaria'), which has, among other functions, to interpret the rules of the agreement. It may be said that the decision offered by the committee, as representative of the parties which bargained the trade agreement, is the best interpretation of all those possible.

698. The particular or case-by-case interpretation – leaving aside of course that made without further argument between employer and employees covered by the agreement – is that made by the courts, mostly by the Labour Courts, to which allegations founded upon collective bargaining clauses are offered in support of either the plaintiff or defendant appearing before them. Supreme Court decisions have made clear more than once that this is the 'true' or 'typical' interpretation and that even if there is a previous general interpretation this does not preclude the court from making its own. Of course, the interpretation made by the courts comes under and has the value generally assigned to, court decisions in the Spanish system of law (Introduction, Chapter 5, §9), including the special importance of Supreme Court decisions handed down in appeals for the unification of judicial doctrine (Part I, Chapter 10, §3(II)), cases. Incidentally, it should be mentioned here that a collective bargaining agreement is a law – not fact – from the point of view of appeals against first instance Labour Court decisions, which makes it possible, relatively frequently for Supreme Court decisions, to interpret collective bargaining agreements.

II. The Rules of Interpretation

699. There is a peculiar problem with the interpretation of the collective bargaining agreements; on the one hand, they are sources of law, and the rules of interpretation of law should be applied to them; on the other hand, they are agreements, that is, they emerge from the will of the parties, and somehow this contractual origin is in the background, and the rules of interpretation of contracts should be also taken into account.

700. Most fortunately both types of rules of interpretation tend to coincide in their meaning and intent, as they are formulated within the venerable Civil Code. The Code allows for both law and contract, and there are four interpretations which are successively applied.

701. The law must be interpreted 'according to the proper sense of the word used' (Article 3.1); if the words used in the contract are clear and there is no doubt about the intent of the parties, the literal sense of the words will prevail (Article 1281). Thus literal interpretation shall be used in the first place if the clauses of the collective bargaining agreement are sufficiently clear.

702. The words of the law must be interpreted 'within their context' (Article 3.1); 'clauses of the contract shall be interpreted one with another, giving to the doubtful ones the meaning that results from their whole' (Article 1285).

For doubtful clauses of the agreement, then, systematic interpretation is called for, and of course, this type of interpretation rejects taking any clause of the agreement out of its context.

703. Laws must be interpreted having in mind 'their historical and legal precedents' (Article 3); 'to ascertain the will of the parties of the contract their coetanous conduct shall be borne in mind' (Article 1282). There is a slight difference here, probably because the history prior to a contract is not usually as prolonged or as well reported as that of an act, for instance. As applied to the collective bargaining agreement the rules command that previous history of collective bargaining within the unit, previous agreements, or more proximately, the story of the negotiation itself, if somehow recorded, of the agreement being interpreted, shall also be taken into consideration in case of doubt. Of course, this is what is usually called the historical interpretation.

704. Lastly law must be interpreted taking care of 'its purposes and spirit' (Article 3) and contracts shall be constructed never forgetting that they subject the parties to 'every consequence that, according to its nature, conforms with good faith, usage, and law' (Article 1258). This 'spirit', whether of the law or of the contract, is a last and fruitful source of interpretation which of course applies to what the parties have collectively bargained for and agreed upon.

705. The much-quoted Article 3 of the Civil Code says that the law shall also be interpreted according to the 'social realities of the time in which they are going to be applied', but this rather novel provision of the Code – it was, introduced in 1974 – seems to apply to Acts of a long duration in which social realities do change; it will not be easy to apply this rule of interpretation to such a short-lived instrument as a labour collective agreement. If reality changes, a new agreement is what is needed, not an adapted interpretation of an old one.

706. Attention should be called here to the general principles of labour law (Introduction, Chapter 5, §9); its use as rules of interpretation – the principle pro operario, mainly – is relatively frequent in the sense already studied.

§8. Other Collective Bargaining Agreements

707. After the promulgation of the WSA, there arose a discussion regarding the legal existence of collective agreements which do not derive from ES rules or do not pay attention to its formalities and proceedings. Article 82 WSA mentions 'collective agreements regulated by the law', which seems implicitly to recognize other types can exist. This type of agreement will exist especially when at least one of the parties does not have the mandatory legitimacy to negotiate according to the WSA rules. Labour court decisions have recognized the existence and the validity of these collective agreements with contractual, not normative, force. These collective agreements are called, in Spain. of 'convenios colectivos extraestatutarios' (extra-statutory collective agreements).

708. Besides that, an 'informal' negotiation between employer and employees' representatives frequently develops in the enterprise about different matters. As we have seen above, since 1994 the law has considerably extended these cases of enterprise negotiations making possible more flexibility in the regulation of certain work conditions. Matters such as employees' classification, professional advancements, working time and changes in the normal conditions of work appear in the WSA as the content of these agreements. Peculiarities of the work centre or enterprise being important to the best regulation of most of these topics, it must be said that this negotiation, more informal but nearer the specific questions, is in many cases the best means by which to regulate them. We must also remember that this 'extended' collective bargaining in the enterprise is explicitly justified by the law itself as a way to obtain a more flexible regulation of work conditions.

It is debated whether these agreements have the same normative force as the 'proper' collective agreements adhering to the WSA rules in §3 and §4. A probable interpretation is that they do not, although, when the collective agreement on a specific matter makes up for the lack of regulation of a certain matter in a collective agreement regulated by law, the conclusion is that it does seem that normative effectiveness should be attributed to it (this supplementary function is what it usually plays on many occasions when the WSA contemplates the possibility of negotiating collective agreements on a specific matter). However, in the event that it is concluded that the collective agreement on a specific matter has an effectiveness that is not normative, but obligatory, we must consider that the conditions accepted by the employer and the employees' representatives are incorporated into the individual labour contracts of the employees concerned.

Chapter 4. Strikes and Lock-Outs

§1. Introduction

709. In the past political system, there was a period in which the law was simply ignorant of strikes and lock-outs; afterwards, the euphemistically called 'collective conflicts' were regulated repeatedly with basic enactments appearing in 1962, 1970, 1975 and 1977. The 1977 regulation is contained in Title I of Royal Decree Act 17/1977, of 4 March, which significantly is entitled (On) The Right to Strike. Compared with other previous regulations, this last one had a more open and progressive position: we must point out the date of the LRRDA: it is the same year as that in which the recuperation of union and association freedom and the first democratic election for a pluralistic Parliament in the so-called democratic pre-constitutional (1975–1978) period.

710. On strikes and lock-outs, the LRRDA established, among other rules, several on legitimation and proceedings to exercise one and another, on the effect of strike and lock-out on the labour contract. It makes a list of illegal strikes, i.e., abuse of the right to strike. In its Title II, the LRRDA lists the proceedings for settlement of collective disputes.

711. The 1978 Constitution, besides the trade union freedom and the right to collective bargaining between employees' and employers' representatives, says in Article 28: 'Employees right to strike is recognized for the defence of their interests. The law which shall rule this right shall establish necessary guarantees in order to assure functioning in the community's essential services.' Several questions are brought up in this article; among them and possibly most important are who are the holders of the right to strike; what scope do the interests defended through the strike have; and which are the services considered essential.

712. The Constitution contains also a general rule which declares abolished 'every law opposed to the Constitution itself'. On the basis of this rule, the question is to know if the LRRDA was or was not in force; the negative opinion was maintained on the basis that regulations and limits contained in the LRRDA over strikes were incompatible with the Constitution's guarantee of the right to strike.

713. In October 1980, an appeal on unconstitutionality was introduced against the LRRDA. The Constitutional Court gave its decision in April 1981: it decided on the unconstitutionality – i.e., the abolition – of several rules of the LRRDA, establishing at the same time the correct interpretation for several others in order to be in accordance with the Constitution itself.

In short, the decision of the Constitutional Court has maintained the LRRDA in force in an important part. But the question is not definitively solved: the integration of the LRRDA in the new constitutional framework continues putting questions, not all of them solved by the decision. Probably, only through a new regulation – the Act which is named by Article 28 of the Constitution – could these difficulties be solved: but parliamentary experience has shown the difficulties of this enactment.

714. The following statement about strikes and lock-outs made on the basis of the LRRDA rules is still in force according to the decision of the Constitutional Court.

§2. The Right to Strike and Its Exercise

715. The provisions of the LRRDA are based upon a distinction, which is sometimes clear and sometimes blurred, between legal strikes (or, if you prefer, proper and due exercise of the right to strike) and illegal strikes (improper or abusive use of same right). The best way to tackle the LRRDA is, first of all, to establish what are legal and what are illegal strikes from a substantive point of view; and then to study what are the procedures of legal strikes, since, of course, the LRRDA does not regulate illegal strikes (however, it will qualify as illegal, strikes in which the procedure is not, at all or in some substantial part, followed). The most important of the effects, first of legal then of illegal strikes will follow.

716. Although not defined by the LRRDA, the strike is generally conceived in the Act as the collective and concerted suspension by the employees of the performance of work due under their labour contracts. An analysis of this definition will reveal five points.

a. The strike consists of a suspension of work, i.e., a refusal by the workers to comply with their basic duty under the contract; according to the LRRDA for the strike to be legal, it has to consist precisely of 'stopping of services by the affected workers'. Activities such as the occupation of the workplace or sit-down strikes, working-to-rule or go-slow strikes and strikes in which employees stop working by departments in rotation or sequence are all illegal strikes precisely because they do not consist of a simple suspension of work.
   Labour Court decisions have stated that these strikes are abusive only when an interruption of work of only some employees has the proven objective of amplifying the effects of the strike.
b. The suspension must be collective which means that the strike is by nature a collective phenomenon which affects a plurality of workers. Throughout the LRRDA it is clear that a strike is meant only to be the suspension of work by a collectivity.
c. The strike is a suspension, not a termination of the contract; the strikers do not have the intention to terminate the contract, but only to interrupt work due under it. Again the LRRDA says that 'the strike does not terminate the labour relationship; during the strike the labour contract will be deemed to be suspended'.

d. This suspension, of which the strike consists, must be concerted and agreed upon. The deliberation can at times be very brief, but it shall exist. The LRRDA required a ballot to be taken by the employees of the work centre, a rule today declared unconstitutional.
e. The suspension is due to the workers' decision which of course distinguishes it from the lock-out. The workers' decision may be based upon many different causes, among them previous attitude of the employer; but the immediate decision, as opposed to the motivation to suspend, must be the employees.

717. Thus generally defined, the LRRDA starts including some additional elements, or excluding others, to delineate with more precision what is meant by a legal strike.

718. Of course, the regulation of the LRRDA refers only to strikes of people who are technically employees, that is persons who work for one or several employers under a labour contract; other types of strikes, if that term may still be used, such as those of independent workers or students, are completely outside the rules of the LRRDA.

719. A different question of course is the legality of the public servants strike, whose relationship with the state or, more general, with the public administration, is not under labour law but administrative law. The LRRDA rules refer – as we have said – only to strikes of persons who work under a labour contract and say nothing about a possible right to strike public servants. Nevertheless, its rules are sometimes applied by analogy.

The decision of the Constitutional Court of 1981 has confirmed this exclusion, but it said nothing about the legality of the strike of this special group of employees. More recently, an Act of 2007, applying to labour conditions of public employees, has recognized their right to strike, although no regulation exists about its proceeding. A limit, however, must be indicated: continuity of the essential services for the community must be preserved. Certain groups of public servants do not have the right to strike, mainly those who have no right to unionize. Nor are public servants of security services entitled to strike.

720. From the point of view of the LRRDA, the strike must have in view employment-connected matters, i.e., it has to be a professional one. If the strike 'is begun or maintained by political motivations or any others alien to the professional interests of the workers affected', the strike is illegal.

The Constitutional Court admits strikes for the defence of general economic or social employees' rights, which includes strikes as a means of pressing public powers in order to obtain better labour conditions; the strict political strike, i.e., with mere political objectives, remains illegal.

721. Typical strikes are those which refer to the relationship between the striking employees and their employer; secondary or sympathetic strikes are in principle illegal strikes; but the wording of the LRRDA is rather cryptic in this respect; the strike is illegal 'when it is a solidarity strike, unless the professional interest of the strikers is affected'. It is plain that some solidarity strikes are legal but there must be some professional connection, besides the sympathy between the old and the new strikers.

The Constitutional Court has introduced some flexibility in the regulation of the solidarity strike, although its wording is not yet sufficiently clear; its decision declares unconstitutional the LRRDA rule which requires that the interest defended through the strike affects, directly, the strikers.

722. Whether or not there is a collective bargaining agreement in force at the time of the strike is examined next by the LRRDA. The strike is illegal if its purpose is to modify or alter labour conditions when the trade agreement is in force. This allows for a legal strike when the reason for that strike is not the modification of what was collectively agreed, but the existence between the parties of the unsolved differences of interpretation or construction about the trade agreement itself. In this case, the strike is illegal only if there is an express clause in the collective agreement that forbids any strike (probably providing at the same time for some mechanism to deal with difference of interpretation) while the agreement is in force.

The decision of the Constitutional Court, so repeatedly quoted, confirms this interpretation; nothing forbids – it says – a strike when the trade agreement is in force if the purpose of the strike is not to modify the agreement itself; it can be to ask for an interpretation of its rules or to demand something that does not imply its modification.

723. An explicit limit of the right to strike in Article 28 of the Constitution is the mandatory maintenance of 'essential services for the community'. Some 'minimum services' must be maintained in these cases. The law does not establish which services are essential. The Constitutional Court has said they are the services which cover rights or goods constitutionally protected (life, health, information, public security, etc.). The state or autonomous regions may fix the services to be maintained in cases of strike thus somewhat limiting the right to strike.

724. Perhaps, all this having been said, we can accept the risk of at least describing what is meant by a 'legal' strike according to the LRRDA; the description will be: a professional strike of employees, which consists of the simple suspension of work, for reasons connected with the professional interests of the strikers, as long as no attempt is made to modify a collective bargaining agreement currently in force. Illegal strikes will be those which do not meet this description.

§3. The Procedure for a Legal Strike

725. The LRRDA subjected the right to strike to a rigorous procedure, first of all establishing some connection between the strike itself and the means provided to resolve it. Second, ascertaining that the strike is in effect the will of at least a majority of the strikers. But it also has some important indirect effects, in the sense that strikes which are initiated or developed out of the proceedings provided for them or are a gross violation of those proceedings, are also illegal and will be treated as such.

726. This is precisely one of the questions more attentively examined by the Constitutional Court in its decision of June 1981. First of all, it declares legal the existence of legal proceedings for the right to strike, but adds that these forms cannot be arbitrary; they must have the aim to protect other goods or rights also protected by the Constitution and cannot be as rigid or as difficult to accomplish in the practice as to make impossible its exercise.

Bearing this in mind, the successive procedural steps provided by the LRRDA and today in force are the following.

a. The right to strike can be decided directly by the interested employees or by their representatives, in this last case shop stewards, work centre councils or trade unions. Thus, both the union strike and the so-called wild-cat strike are legal.
b. The decision to strike shall be notified to the employer and to the administrative authority, this notice, in writing, shall express the 'objectives' of the strike and when the strike will begin, as well as the composition of the 'strike committee' of which more will be said later. The notice must be given at least five days (ten days if a public service is to be affected) before the strike starts.
c. As to the development of the strike itself, nothing is said, except of course to be a legal strike it must consist of a simple suspension of work. But for some ancillary activities, there are rules in the LRRDA mainly:
   - The strike committee, and the employer, are under a duty to negotiate with a view to ending the strike by solving the problems out of which it arose.
   - The strike committee is under a duty to guarantee the rendering of services of work needed for the security of the work centre, and the prompt resumption of work when the strike ends. Employer and strike committee will agree on the employees who should perform these services.
   - The strike can be the subject of 'publicity in a pacific way', which means that peaceful picketing is allowed. However, unpeaceful or coercive picketing will come under the Penal Code as an offence against the right to work.
   - Strikers can ask for funds to support themselves during the strike, provided this is done 'without any coercion'.
   - The right to work of those workers who do not want to participate in the strike will be respected, says the LRRDA; this rule is in perfect congruence with the idea that the right to strike is an individual one.
d. There is no special provision for the end of the strike. As there is a duty to negotiate during the strike, it is assumed that eventually some agreement will be reached, and the LRRDA states that such an agreement will have 'the same effect as a collective bargaining agreement', which actually it is. But the strike can end in practical terms, so to speak, without any agreement, because the workers resumed work. Actually, with or without an agreement, the strike does not end until the resumption of work.

§4. THE EFFECTS OF THE LEGAL STRIKE

727. Let us make a distinction between the basic and ancillary effects of the legal strike as provided by the LRRDA and as developed by court rulings.

I. Basic Effects

728. The basic effects of the legal strike are of course the suspension of the labour contract and, consequently, of the reciprocal duties to work and to pay wages; the most important Article 6.1 and 2 of the LRRDA develops this principle in the following way:

- The legal strike or, to use the LRRDA words, 'the exercise of the right to strike' does not terminate the labour relationship.
- During the strike the labour contract is suspended; consequently, the employee will not have a right to his wages; and consequently of course the employer has no right to the services of the employee. Workers entrusted with security duties are exempted from these provisions.
- The legal strike is not just a cause for dismissal. Dismissals attempted are unjustified dismissals.
- But sanctions, including dismissal, are possible during the strike if the employee commits an act or indulges in conduct which will be considered a justified cause for dismissal independently of the suspension of the contract.

II. Ancillary Effects

729. During the strike the employer cannot employ workers who were not in his service at the beginning of the strike to take the place of striking employees. Strikebreakers are thus forbidden in legal strikes. But he can employ any workers for security services if those named do not report for work. Act 14/1994 expressly forbids to employ workers of temporary work firms to replace strikers.

Strikers have no right to unemployment benefits during the strike. During the strike, the payment of social security contributions from the employer and employee is suspended.

§5. EFFECTS OF ILLEGAL STRIKES

730. The effects of illegal strikes are not clearly established by the LRRDA and therefore must be extracted from what is provided for legal strikes. There are three basic effects:

- the illegal strike does not by itself terminate the labour contract, but only suspends it;
- the illegal strike gives cause to the employer to justly dismiss the employee;

– but simple participation in an illegal strike is not in itself enough to justify a dismissal; it has to be an 'active participation', a rather nebulous expression which is probably directed against the organizers of the illegal strike.

731. A decision by an employer to dismiss an employee because of active participation in an illegal strike must be effected forthwith, or within a reasonably short time in accordance with the circumstances. The employee is further precluded from dismissals, no matter how illegal the strike has been and how active the participation, if the employees have accepted and complied with his offer to resume work at a certain date and on certain conditions; this offer if accepted will be deemed to comprise implicitly a general promise neither to dismiss nor to otherwise discipline.

732. As to the ancillary effects, there seems to be no difference between legal and illegal strikes. As to social security benefits the consequences are probably similar to both types of strikes: the duty to maintain the security services at the work site without any change, except for the role of the strike committee (which will probably not even exist during an illegal strike). It is difficult to think about forbidding peaceful picketing even if the strike is illegal, and the same can be said about a non-coercive collection of funds.

733. Before leaving the effects of legal and illegal strikes the observation should be made that nobody, it seems, has jurisdiction to define it. The Labour Courts no longer determine at the outset or during its development whether a strike is legal or illegal. A decision in this sense will only occur in dealing with the effects if someone concerned goes to court; for instance, a dismissed employee complaining about his dismissal, whose justification or lack of it will depend, *inter alia*, on whether the strike was legal or illegal. But if this does not happen, and it does not necessarily have to happen, the strike will begin and end without anybody knowing, or expressly caring for, any declaration about the quality of the strike. Needless to say, many strikes belong in practice to this type of factual strike.

734. Finally, it should be noted that Spanish law classifies as administrative penalty, punishable by substantial administrative fines on occasions, certain behaviours related to the exercise of strike action – *see*, Organic Act 4/2015, of 30 March, on the Protection of Citizens' Security. Similarly, the current Criminal Code criminalizes certain behaviours related to the participation in a strike, as criminal behaviours – particularly the Article 315 of the Criminal Code.

§6. Lock-Outs

735. There is no necessity to delve into the definition or characteristics of a lock-out. It is sufficient to say that its seeming parallelism with the strike is not as clear as it was in the past; strikes are clearly an autonomous right of the employees, while lock-outs tend to be conceived now as a reaction of the employer admissible only in very definite and precise conditions and situations the presence of which is strictly necessary for the lock-out to be considered legal.

736. In the current regulation regarding the lock-out we may see a similar situation to that regarding the strike: the LRRDA rules have suffered the impact of the Constitution rules. The 1981 decision of the Constitutional Court has also considered this important question.

737. As we have said, the parallelism between strike and lock-out is relative and doubtful. The Constitution says that 'the employees' right to strike is recognized for the defence of their interests' and offers this right a special protection as one of the 'essential rights and public liberties' of the citizens. On the contrary, the lock-out is not even named by the Constitution: it mentions only the employers' right 'to take measures of collective conflict', which is not a very clear expression; however, this right is not under the special protection, abovementioned, that covers the essential rights and liberties.

738. The decision of the Constitutional Court rejects the parallel in the regulation of strike and lock-out. This refusal is made, first, on the basis of the right to work: lock-out, affecting strikers and non-strikers, seriously violates the right to work of the latter. Second, it affirms that the guarantee of the right to strike tends to re-establish the balance between 'parties with no-equal economic power'; to recognize a parallel right to lock-out will signify as much as to recognize 'a greater dose of power to a person who previously has power'. Regulation of strike and lock-out, concludes the Constitutional Court, cannot be the same.

739. Rules of the LRRDA, as interpreted by the Constitutional Court, are the basis of the regulation in force about the lock-out. There is a distinction between legal and illegal lock-out.

I. Legal Lock-Outs

740. The LRRDA authorizes the employer to proceed with a lock-out in the case of a strike or other 'irregularity in the performance of work', when at least one of the following conditions exists:

- danger of, or actual, violence to persons or damage to property;
- sit-down strikes or occupation of the place of work; or a clear and present danger that this may happen;
- a volume of absenteeism or irregularities in the work which 'gravely impede the normal work processes'.

741. The Constitutional Court's decision accepts the legality of this regulation but submits it to two conditions. First, the employer's measure cannot render ineffective the right to strike; in other words, 'it cannot be considered legal that a simple civil right hinders an essential right'. Second, the legal lock-out must be conceived as a 'policy faculty' in order to ensure the integrity of persons, goods and equipment, which is limited to the time necessary to end the causes of the damage and re-establish normal working.

742. The employer who proceeds with a lock-out, because of the presence of any of these circumstances, must notify the fact within twelve hours to the administrative authority; but the decision to close is the employer's and is applicable only for the time necessary to remove the causes of the lock-out and to ensure the normal resumption to work.

743. If time passes without a re-opening of the worksite by the employer, of his own accord or on the intervention of a petition to that end from the employees, the owner shall re-open if he is so advised by the administrative authority, at the date or within the time fixed by it.

744. If he does not re-open the lock-out will be illegal from this moment on, with effects which will be studied below.

The effects of the legal lock-out are the same generally, both basic and ancillary, as those of the legal strike.

II. Illegal Lock-Outs

745. In the LRRDA regulation, a lock-out will be deemed to be illegal if it is decided without mediation of any of the causes just studied for legal lock-outs. Or, if initially legal, the lock-out is continued after the advice to cease is issued by the administrative authority.

746. In view of the Constitutional Court's decision, whose main principles have just been described, it is clear that a lock-out is illegal when it goes against the right to strike or when it goes beyond the simple 'policy goal' of the employer to ensure the integrity of persons, goods and equipment.

747. From the point of view of the employees again the effects are the same as those of the legal strike, but with the extremely important addition that wages – compensation in lieu of, and of the same amount as wages – are due during an illegal lock-out.

748. The employer, besides his duty to pay wages, can be sanctioned with administrative fines.

The sanction of course can be appealed before the Courts. As with the strikes, and for the same or similar reasons, there will be many cases of factual lock-outs without any decision about their legality or illegality.

Chapter 5. Settlement of Industrial Disputes: Protection of Vital Needs

§1. Introduction

749. First let us consider the terminology: 'industrial dispute' is another way of referring to collective labour conflicts; the distinction between them and individual labour conflicts was studied in Part I, Chapter 10, §1 and §3. Since that chapter was dedicated to the settlement of (individual) disputes (or conflicts) we can concentrate now on the study of the settlement of industrial (or collective) disputes (or conflicts).

750. The matter will be studied under the following headings:

- settlement by the parties themselves through direct negotiation;
- settlement by the parties with the aid of a conciliator or mediator;
- settlement by an arbitrator chosen by the parties;
- settlement by a public arbitrator;
- settlement by compulsory arbitration or court decision.

751. In this matter too, regulation of the LRRDA has been revised by the Constitutional Court; its 1981 decision has maintained most of the rules of the LRRDA and declared the non-constitutionality of several of them.

752. In January 1996, a national agreement between the most representative unions and employers' associations was signed in order to establish a non-judicial system of industrial dispute settlement. The agreement, renewed several times after that date, includes mediation and arbitration proceedings. The last agreement signed in this area was the VI Agreement on Autonomous Settlement of Labour Disputes in 2020. This practice, the result of social dialogue, has also been replicated at the level of the Spanish Autonomous Regions, with successive agreements being signed on the matter for these territorial areas in these successive years.

§2. Settlement by Direct Negotiation

753. There is no need to say that this is both the simplest and the most frequently used system for resolving industrial disputes. The parties themselves, usually the employees through their representatives, reach an agreement that puts an end to the dispute.

754. Perhaps because of its simplicity, and perhaps because a legal regulation will tend to unduly formalize proceedings which should remain open and flexible, this type of settlement, its frequency notwithstanding, is the least regulated. The LRRDA does not ignore this way of solving the dispute; as was already said (Chapter 4, §3) the employer and the employees during the strike are under a duty to negotiate to solve it; and as will be seen, the Social Jurisdiction Act (SJA) says that proceedings before the Labour Court in industrial disputes will be closed once it is reported to the court that the parties have reached an agreement; but in neither case is there any regulation about the negotiation itself. Still, there is a very clear rule about its effects: the agreement so reached has 'the value of a collectively bargained agreement' (LRRDA Article 8).

755. The reference to the negotiated settlement both in the LRRDA and in the SJA contemplates a situation of a strike or, at least, an open and declared dispute. When such is not the case – and leaving aside that the collective bargaining agreement itself can be considered a way of settling a labour dispute – the law provides two instruments for reaching a settlement by negotiation. Both of these have been referred to already and, consequently, just a brief mention here will be sufficient.

a. The work centre council, as stated above (Chapter 2, §3(III)) has the function of watching over the fulfilment of the labour, social security and employment laws, and of agreements and enterprise practices in force. On the basis of this function, it can initiate legal proceedings before the employer, from which a claim shall normally result; the end of this claim may be an agreement which signifies the settlement of the dispute. However, many of the 'consultation functions' of the work centre council indicated above can establish an agreement between employer and employees' representatives, bringing a settlement of the dispute which has arisen in those cases.
b. Part of the mandatory content of a collectively bargained agreement is the institution of one Joint Committee of the Agreement ('Comisión paritaria del convenio') to solve questions which derive from the application of the trade agreement. Again, a solution reached within these committees as to a trade dispute is a negotiated solution. Although this type of negotiated settlement is thought of only for juridical or legal disputes – and not economic ones – some importance is to be attached to it even in these cases, because what actually happens within the committee is that the process of negotiation is continuous after its appearance in the trade agreement itself; especially if, as often happens, the stipulations of the trade agreement are not as clear as necessary for the guidance of the faithful – perhaps because if they tried to be clear enough there would have been no statement at all, i.e., no agreement would have been reached – and so the parties leave the matter for further and, if not as glorious, surely more peaceful moments.

756. Let us repeat that besides using the two 'instruments' just mentioned, the parties can enter into any type of informal or impromptu negotiations and they do so occasionally. It is not unusual to find among the facts in a Labour Court decision that an informal, even an oral, 'agreement' was obtained by the parties or their representatives on such and such a day, about such and such matter, and in such and such way, in good faith, and so they both must stand by it; pacta sunt servanda generally in collective labour relations, even if some authorities will not agree entirely with the proposition.

757. The LRRDA accepts that the parties of the collective agreement can bargain and reach 'complementary rules' to settle a dispute; through them, it is clear that the parties can empower the 'committee of the agreement' to carry out any function, create another different commission or establish other different proceedings for the settlement of the disputes, including direct negotiation.

§3. Settlement by Conciliation or Mediation

758. The difference between conciliation, in which the third party intervenes to approach the parties in conflict, and mediation, in which the third party is empowered to make proposals and offer solutions, is, of course, well known in Spanish legal literature. The point is that in Spanish law both institutions appear always jointly and, as a matter of course, it is understood that the one who can conciliate can also mediate, and vice versa.

759. Two types of conciliation-mediation are formally provided for and respectively entrusted by the LRRDA to labour inspectors and to the administrative authority. In the national agreement mentioned above a specific mediation proceeding is provided.

760. Labour Inspectors have among their legal functions the duties of 'mediation in collective labour conflicts'. And LRRDA Article 9 says also that the Labour Inspector may mediate in a trade dispute from the moment at which the strike is notified to the administrative authority. The Labour Inspector may do that of his own accord or if called in by the parties.

761. In practice this type of conciliation and/or mediation is frequent; and in practice too, the Labour Inspector may and does meet the parties, or their representatives, jointly or separately, and offer his proposals for the solution of the dispute.

762. The administrative authority must try to conciliate and/or mediate in the dispute at a precise moment to which reference will be made later.

763. The mediator so nominated can convoke the parties of the dispute in order to obtain the necessary information about it. In a short space of time, he must submit his proposals to the parties.

764. Any agreement reached through conciliation or mediation has the same effects, says the LRRDA, as a collectively bargained agreement. And the collectively bargained agreement, however, can provide any reasonable system of conciliation and/or mediation, although clauses with such content have been most infrequent in the past; certainly the 'agreement committee' must be created but it usually functions through direct negotiations, without the help of any outside conciliator or mediator.

765. The mediation proceeding provided by the 2012 and following agreements is regulated with some detail. It is conceived as a voluntary proceeding, or as obligatory when one of the parties asks for it.

766. In a majority of autonomous regions some agreements between the most representative unions and employers' associations have established mediation proceedings for the settlement of economic and juridical disputes in this territorial scope.

§4. SETTLEMENT BY VOLUNTARY ARBITRATION

767. This type of settlement means that the conflicting parties agree, through an arbitration agreement, to submit their differences to one or several arbitrators nominated by both parties. Although the initiation of proceedings has a conventional nature, the decision of the arbitrator does not have such a nature, i.e., it is a mandatory decision from a third person neutral to both parties.

The LRRDA gives some rules on voluntary arbitration. The national agreement mentioned above has established a specific proceeding for it.

768. LRRDA establishes that the parties can nominate one or several arbitrators: in the second case, they must act conjointly. The arbitrator has a very short period in which to make his decision, five days; the decision has the same effect as a collective bargaining agreement. No more procedural rules are given by the LRRDA, that allow great flexibility according to the circumstances of the case.

769. We must remember here the faculty of the parties of a trade agreement, as established by LRRDA and WSA, to establish an arbitration proceeding to resolve the disputes arising from the application of its rules. Arbitrator or arbitrators shall be the persons nominated in the agreement or according to its rules. The difference between this case and the above-mentioned is the following: in the case now studied the arbitration contract is previous to the appearance of the dispute and general for every dispute arising while the agreement is in force.

770. Following the 2020 national agreement rules, arbitration proceedings are initiated by the two parties, choosing the name or names of arbitrators from a list established by unions and employers' associations. The arbitrator gives his decision within a very short term; this decision may be appealed before the Labour Court only in certain cases (decision over questions not submitted to arbitration or dictated beyond the fixed term, among others). Strikes and lock-outs are forbidden during this proceeding.

771. This conventional system for the settlement of industrial disputes, including mediation and arbitration proceedings, is today in practice followed by a preference for the system established by the LRRDA.

§5. SETTLEMENT BY PUBLIC ARBITRATION

772. The LRRDA established – with precedents in the previous legislation on settlements of industrial disputes – an arbitration conferred on the administrative authority; it was a compulsory arbitration, up to a certain point. The decision of the Constitutional Court of June 1981, repeatedly quoted, declared it unconstitutional, assuming that it was against the collective bargaining right guaranteed by the Constitution.

773. When the decision to submit the dispute to public arbitration is made by the parties, no defect of unconstitutionality exists. This procedure is valid both for economic disputes and for the application of rules disputes. In the LRRDA plan, this procedure is conceived as an alternative to strike: if the employees have initiated it, they cannot strike; on the contrary, if the employer initiates it, and employees strike the proceeding must be suspended.

774. The LRRDA regulates the proceeding with some detail, through the following procedural steps.

775. First, the submission to arbitration must be made in writing by the representative of the employees, or by the employer or employers or their representatives; it shall include the identification of the parties, the facts of the dispute and the petition in relation to them.

776. Second, the administrative authority sends a copy, within twenty-four hours of the submission, to the other party and sets a date, within the three following days, for a hearing of both parties.

777. Third, in the hearing the administrative authority tries to conciliate or mediate in the dispute (this is the moment at which his activity as conciliator or mediator appears); also, at the hearing, the parties may try to submit the dispute to one or several, acting jointly – private arbitrators appointed by them.

778. Fourth, if there is no agreement on either of those alternative ways, then the proceedings divide according to the nature of the dispute to follow either of these two possible procedures:

a. If the dispute is a 'legal' or juridical one, that is, if there is a dispute 'about the interpretation of pre-existing governmental or collectively bargained rule', the administrative authority sends the case, with his report, to the Labour Court (the SJA contains in effect special rules for these special proceedings). The Labour Court arranges a new hearing for both parties and hands down its decision – which can be appealed – no later than three days after the hearing. In addition to the short length of the hearing, these types of judicial proceedings take preference in time over any other submitted to the Court and actually are decided by the Courts, both in first instance and in appeal, with the utmost rapidity. As stated earlier the Court dismisses the case if it is reported that, prior to its own decision, the parties to the dispute have solved it by agreement.

b. If the dispute is an 'economic' one, that is, the object is to establish new labour conditions – a type of dispute that is only possible when there is no collective labour agreement in force – there is no further solution in the LRRDA. The administrative authority had the faculty to decide the dispute, giving a written decision, but this faculty was declared unconstitutional by the Constitutional Court. We must think that the parties at this moment can decide the continuity of the proceeding by negotiation, arbitration or mediation.

779. In the autonomous regions with faculties in the settlement of industrial disputes, the competence studied above obviously pertains to their own administrative organs.

§6. Compulsory Arbitration

780. 'Compulsory arbitration' is only provided for in the LRRDA if the Council of Ministers, following the advice of the Minister of Labour, decides in cases of strikes whose duration, consequences, (intransigent) position of the parties or grievous effect on the national economy, develop into a situation which so commands. Actually, in this way, compulsory arbitration is resorted to when a vital need of the community has to be protected.

781. The Constitutional Court decision of June 1981 has declared that this type of compulsory arbitration for exceptional cases is not unconstitutional; being compulsory, states the Courts, it is arbitration up to a certain point, provided the impartiality of the arbitrator is guaranteed. The Supreme Court for its own part has admitted this type of compulsory arbitration decided by authorities of autonomous regions in disputes of regional scope.

782. The LRRDA gives no procedural rules in this case of arbitration. We may think that the Government, taking its decision, can give the rules; those of the public arbitration which have been studied earlier can be applied in default of special regulation.

783. The LRRDA established also for this type of strike of special gravity the governmental faculty to order a cooling-off period of up to two months, during which work must be resumed. The Constitutional Court has declared that this faculty is unconstitutional, because it is a non-admissible obstacle to the exercise of an essential right, this is, the right to strike.

Selected Bibliography

In making the following selection, on the whole, attention has been paid to both the generality and the modernity of the books; trying to accomplish the rather difficult task of making a selection among the formidable and increasing literature on labour and industrial relations topics.

Introductions

A fairly common type of book is the 'Introduction' which studies the social and economic backgrounds of labour law and industrial relations, and their historical development; perhaps with indications of comparative labour law by way of setting the Spanish developments within the general trend of Western European and Latin American countries. To this category belong the following:

M. Alonso Olea, *Introducción al Derecho del Trabajo* (Introduction to Labour Law), 7th edn, Madrid 2013 (Civitas).

General Books

Full and complete analysis of Spanish Labour Law – comprising both its individual and collective sides – is provided by the courses and treatises of labour law, generally prepared for University use. In both the Faculties of Law and Economic Sciences, labour law and/or industrial relations is a mandatory course. To this category belong the following:

M. Alonso Olea and M.E. Casas, *Derecho del Trabajo* (Labour Law), 27th edn, Madrid, 2010 (Thomson/Civitas).

J. Cruz Villalón, *Compendio de Derecho del Trabajo* (Labour Law Abridgement) 17th edn, 2024 (Tecnos).

J.I. Garcia Ninet et al., *Manual de Derecho Sindical* (Trade Union Law Handbook), 4th edn, 2017 (Atelier).

I. García-Perrote, *Manual de Derecho del Trabajo* (Labour Law Handbook), 14th edn, Valencia, 2024 (Tirant lo Blanch).

A. Martin Valverde, and J. García Murcia, *Derecho del Trabajo* (Labour Law), 33rd edn, Madrid, 2024 (Tecnos).

J.R. Mercader Uguina, A. de la Puebla, and F.J. Gómez Abelleira: *Lecciones de Derecho del Trabajo* (Lessons of Labour Law), 17th edn, Valencia, 2024 (Tirant lo Blanch).

J.L. Monereo, C. Molina and M.N. Moreno Vida, *Manual de Derecho del Trabajo* (Labour Law Handbook), 22th edn, Granada, 2024 (Comares).

J.L. Monereo, C. Molina and M.N. Moreno, *Manual de Derecho Sindical* (Trade Union Law Handbook), 12th edn, Granada, 2017 (Comares).
A. Montoya, *Derecho del Trabajo* (Labour Law), 45th edn, Madrid 2024 (Tecnos).
A. Ojeda, *Compendio de Derecho Sindical* (Trade Union Law Abridgement), 4th edn, Madrid, 2020 (Tecnos).
M.C. Palomeque, *Derecho Sindical* (Trade Union Law), 5th edn, Madrid, 2020 (Udima).
J.M. Ramirez, J. Garcia Ortega and T. Sala, *Curso básico de Derecho del Trabajo* (Labour Law Basic Course), 20th edn, Valencia, 2024 (Tirant lo Blanch).
T. Sala, *Derecho Sindical* (Trade Union Law), 4th edn, Valencia, 2022 (Tirant lo Blanch).

Procedure

A treatment of labour disputes specially referring to the system of, and proceedings before Labour Courts, can be found in:

I. Albiol, C.L. Alfonso Mellado, and A. Blasco Pellicer, *Derecho Procesal Laboral* (Procedural Labour Law), 11th edn, Valencia, 2015 (Tirant lo Blanch).
M. Alonso Olea and R. Ma Alonso Garcia, *Derecho Procesal del Trabajo* (Procedural Labour Law), 16th edn, Madrid, 2010 (Thomson/Civitas).
J.L. Monereo et altri, *Manual de Derecho Procesal Laboral* (Procedural Labour Law Handbook), 5th dn, Madrid, 2020 (Tecnos).
A. Montoya Melgar et altri, *Curso de Procedimiento Laboral* (Course of Procedural Labour Law), 12th edn, Madrid, 2019 (Tecnos).

Social Security

Just to complete the picture, and although they do not properly belong here, reference is made to books on Social Security, among them:

J. López Gandía and J.F. Blasco Lahoz, *Curso de Seguridad Social* (Social Security Course), 15th edn, Valencia, 2023 (Tirant lo Blanch).
S. González Ortega and S. Barcelón Cobedo, *Introducción al Derecho de la Seguridad Social* (Introduction to Social Security Law), 18th edn, Valencia, 2024 (Tirant lo Blanch).
J. Gorelli et altri, *Lecciones de Seguridad Social* (Lessons of Social Security), 14th edn, Madrid, 2024 (Tecnos).
J.L. Monereo Pérez, C. Molina Navarrete, and R. Quesada Segura, *Manual de Seguridad Social* (Social Securitye Handbook), 20th edn, Granada, 2024 (Comares).

Monographs

It is not possible to give even a selection of monographs, which are extremely abundant on almost every topic. Most of the general books mentioned in the preceding paragraphs include complete references of these monographs.

A catalogue from law publishing universities and private publishing houses (Tecnos; Bosch; Akal; Ariel; Tirant lo Blanch; Aranzadi La Ley, Marcial Pons; Trotta; Comares; McGraw Hill; Colex, Bomarzo, Laborum, for instance) will undoubtedly include a numerous list of labour law titles. Public institutions, such as Instituto de Estudios Constitucionales, the Consejo Económico Social and the

Publishing Service of the Ministry of Labour and Social Economy also have a number of titles on labour law in their catalogues.

Periodicals and Reviews

Lastly the most important periodicals dealing with Labour Law and Industrial Relations problems are:

Actualidad laboral (Labour Law of Today), published by Edersa (until 2014).

Derecho de las Relaciones Laborales (Law of the Labour Relations), published by Lefebre El Derecho until 2020.

Labos. Revista de Derecho del Trabajo y Protección Social (Labos.Journal of Labour Law and Social Protection), published by Carlos III University.

Revista Crítica de Relaciones de Trabajo (Critical Journal of Labour Relations), published by Laborum.

Revista Española de Derecho del Trabajo (Review of Spanish Labour Law), published by Thomson-Reuters Aranzadi.

Revista de Política Social (Social Policy Review), quarterly publication of the Instituto de Estudios Constitucionales (former Instituto de Estudios Politicos) (until 1985).

Revista de Trabajo (Labour Review), published by the Ministry of Labour and Social Security (until 1996).

Revista Doctrinal Aranzadi Social (Doctrinal Review Aranzadi Social), published by Thomson-Reuters Aranzadi until 2013.

Revista General de Derecho del Trabajo y de la Seguridad Social (General Journal of Labour and Social Security Law) published by Iustel.

Relaciones Laborales (Labour Law Relations), published by La Ley (until 2014).

Revista del Ministerio de Trabajo y Economía Social (Ministry of Labour and Social Economy Review).

Revista de Derecho Social (Social Law Review), published by 'Bomarzo'.

Temas laborales (Labour Themes), published by the Consejo Andaluz de Relaciones Laborales (Junta de Andalucía).

Trabajo y Derecho (Labour and Law), published by Woltes Kluwer.

Tribuna Social (Social Tribune), published by CISS (until 2010).

For any type of statistical data the standard work is Anuario Estadístico de España, published annually by the Instituto Nacional de Estadística, Madrid.

Table of Court Decisions

Court decisions are extremely important in an approach to Labour Law; the best-known reports are those published by publishers Aranzadi La Ley. Also by Aranzadi, the Repertorio de Sentencias del Tribunal Central de Trabajo (Report of Central Labour Court decisions) until 1990. It may be also of interest the consultation in the case-law database of the Centre for Judicial Documentation, in www.poderjudicial.es/search/indexAN.jsp

Decisions of the Constitutional Court are published in the *Boletín Oficial del Estado*. Report of its labour and Social Security decisions in *Jurisprudencia Laboral en el Tribunal Constitucional* (Labour Jurisprudence in the Constitutional Court) (ed. I. Garcia Ninet), I (1981–1988), II (1989–1993), Valencia 1995 (Publisher: Tirant lo Blanch). Yearly commentaries in M. Alonso Olea, A. Montoya et al., *Jurisprudencia Constitucional de Trabajo y Seguridad Social* (Consitutional Jurisprudence of Labour and Social Security) (29 vols., Civitas, 1984–2011).

More recently, the publication service of the *Boletín Oficial del Estado* (Official State Bulletin) offers on the Internet, and freely available, the *Revista de Jurisprudencia Laboral* (Journal of Labour Jurisprudence), where experts periodically comment on significant sentences handed down throughout the year by different Spanish courts and the Court of Justice of the European Union. Likewise, and since 2019, it has published an *Anuario de Jurisprudencia Laboral* (Yearbook of Labour Jurisprudence), where the hundred most significant sentences in the different levels of jurisdiction, both social, constitutional, and community, are analyzed, again by different experts.

Table of Legislation

The primary source of knowledge of the acts, regulations, etc. is the Boletín Oficial del Estado (Official State Bulletin) published daily, except Sundays, by the State Stationery Office (www.boe.es). But the Bulletin also publishes an enormous amount of material which is not 'law'; so the attention of the reader should be addressed to Part I of the Bulletin with the heading Disposiciones Generales (General Norms).

These *Disposiciones Generales* are again published by Aranzadi La Ley on Internet.

There are several good abridgements with the basic labour law norms, among them:

J.M. Goerlich Peset and A. Blasco Pellicer, *Normas laborales básicas*, 21 th end, Valencia, 2024 (Tirant lo Blanch).

A.V. Sempere and G. Rodríguez Iniesta, *Legislación laboral y de Seguridad Social* (Labour Law and Social Security Legislation), 31st edn, Pamplona, 2023 (Thomson-Reuters Aranzadi).

M. Rodriguez-Piñero *et altri*, *Legislación laboral básica* (Basic Labour Law Legislation), 26th edn, Madrid, 2024 (Tecnos).

Index

The numbers here refer to paragraph numbers.

Index

www.ingramcontent.com/pod-product-compliance
Lightning Source LLC
LaVergne TN
LVHW011133300926
849160LV00008B/630